"This book has the inspirational edge of a Dale Carnegie piece and the moral and spiritual backbone of the book of James. It is a sermon on leadership, not a theoretical, ivory tower polemic. It is a must read for anyone attempting to be a leader and for those who sense the need to lead but lack the courage to do so!"

— Julian J. Champion - *Caribbeans for Christ*
Atlanta, GA

"An excellent work…one of the two best I have ever read on Christian leadership. Noah thank you for enduring the process and writing of it!"

— Steve Martin - *Derek Prince Ministries.*

"Powerful work…Noah has offered superb clarity and discernment on the way God regards the leadership issue, both in Christian and secular circles."

— Dennis Matangira - *Wachovia Securities Inc.*

"…powerful reading. At a time when the church desperately needs leaders at all levels, Noah Manyika, with much insight and wisdom, has written a critically important book. It is extremely biblical. It is practical. It is real. It will change the lives of those who have a calling to spiritual leadership."

— Byron Wicker - *Senior Pastor*
River Life Fellowship, NC

"With the applied logic, craftsmanship and inspired passion reminiscent of the classical artisan and follower of Christ who crafted the New Testament argument that Christ was the promised Messiah, Manyika challenges us to make the essential connection between unconditional submission and mission, and to rise to the virtue of availability."

     – Dr. Jameson Kurasha – *Chairman: Department of Religious Studies, Classics and Philosophy University of Zimbabwe*

Visiting Professor of Philosophy Houghton College NY Professor of African Philosophy and Religion Greenville College, IL

Al,

Many blessings as you serve Him.

In Christ,

Noah Manyika

the CHALLENGE
of LEADERSHIP

NOAH MANYIKA

UPLINK
PUBLISHING

Charlotte, North Carolina

the CHALLENGE *of* LEADERSHIP

Published by:
Uplink Publishing
P.O. Box 32454
Charlotte, NC 28232
U.S.A.

info@UplinkPublishing.com

Cover Design by CASAJULIE
www.casajulie.com

ISBN, 0-9755985-0-3   (paperback edition)
ISBN, 0-9755985-1-1   (e-book edition)

DEDICATION

*My wife Phillis and our three children Danielle, Rahab
and Kennedy have been fellow travelers and worthy
companions on the journey that inspired this work.
To them I dedicate this book.*

CONTENTS

ACKNOWLEDGMENTS

I want to thank the following for their invaluable counsel and input during the editing phase of this book:

Byron Wicker, Julian Champion, Aileen Lockhart, Steve Martin, Dennis & Girlie Matangira, Angela DeBoer, Drs. Jameson & Primrose Kurasha, Dimeji Onafuwa and Doug & Ann Murdock. Special thanks to my wife Phillis who has a special gift for completing my thoughts, and who is an unacknowledged source of many of the ideas in this book, and also to Val and Ruth Exis for believing in the project.

While this book bears my name as its author, and the womb of my spirit was where the ideas expressed here were incubated, there are many who were responsible for planting the seeds. We are set on a certain course by those who accept the responsibility to bring us into this world. It is from them that we also get our first understanding of the challenge and responsibility of leadership. I owe a great debt of gratitude to my parents as well as to those I have encountered in the journey of my life who had a life brick to lay: family, teachers, friends and fellow workers in Christ, including those who stoked the fires of the furnace to ensure that I would emerge from it with a word to give.

And to a special group at the Charlotte International Church - you have "endured" much of the teaching in this book. Thank you for your love and prayers and all the support over the years.

INTRODUCTION

The purpose of this book is to inspire you to respond to the challenge of leadership and to provide the truth that will enable you to endure the journey.

The culture of our times demands that we explain the leadership journey in concise, symmetrical success formulae and present it in neat marketable packages. The truth is that some of the most compelling leadership journeys and profiles are hardly pretty.

At the same time, in our effort not to smooth the edges or to offer a neat alternative paradigm, we must avoid the error that equates ugliness with profundity and dismisses every neat paradigm as being shallow and contrived. The intent of this work is to present the reality of the leadership journey, rather than to argue for meaningful ugliness.

Hopefully this book will help you gain the courage to respond to the challenges of our time and the understanding to travel the journey God's way. The end of each chapter provides you with an opportunity to reflect on what you have read. Included also at the end of the book is a study guide which I trust will be a valuable tool for group discussion.

Noah Manyika
Charlotte, NC, USA
July 2004

ONE

Man Interrupted

*Human nature demands
that we build a bridge
over the rushing river
of God's purpose
so we can continue walking
on the sure ground of our own plans,
but the call of God directs us
to step in and be swept away.*

*Great leaders achieve success
by staying the course of
God's detour and
setting aside their own plans
to follow God's.*

For months, I wrote like one possessed. At that rate, the manuscript would be ready for the publisher within six months. Three months into the project with seventy five percent of the writing done, disaster struck. My mind suddenly went blank. For several days I could barely manage a paragraph, down from a daily output of about two thousand words. Thinking that all I needed to get the juices flowing again was to get away from the project for a week or so, I took a break. When I returned to my computer after a few weeks, I began to panic when after several hours, all I had written was a line or two.

During a visit with our family, an out of town friend only made it worse.

"You know that book needs to be published".

"It needs to be finished first" I thought to myself.

Several months later I sat at my desk and typed out the first thing that came to my spirit: *Leadership. The challenge of leadership. The call to leadership.*

That was not the next chapter of the book I was supposed to finish. I followed the thought:

...almost every call to leadership constitutes a detour from the life-path we plan and project for ourselves. It is an interjection, a rude disruption of a well-scripted narrative. We hear God's call as we hear a heckler, and respond to Him accordingly: we just want Him to shut up and let us go on.

This book is the result of the detour I took following that thought. Many self-serving books have been written about leadership. The stories therein often center on human genius, on our ability to plan and to execute the plan to arrive at the desired outcome. A study of God's great leaders reveals that few of them ever planned for the greatness they achieved. Very few became successful as a result of a well-scripted, step-by-step plan for their lives. Instead, they allowed themselves to be interrupted.

They heard God's call, which almost always comes from left field. They responded even when the call took them away from the course they had charted for themselves.   Most were not always willing to detour, learning willingness and obedience as they went along. Greatness came when they set aside their own plans to follow God's.

The Scriptures tell us of Noah who turned away from everything to build an ark to preserve a remnant for God according to His instructions.   His greatness came not out of the execution of a great personal plan, but because he allowed himself to be diverted by God (Genesis 6-7).

Joseph became a great leader in Egypt because he stayed the course of a detour that began with him being sold by his jealous brothers to Midianite traders (Genesis 37:28-36).   Upon arrival in Egypt, the Midianites sold him to Potiphar, one of Pharaoh's officers.   While serving in Potiphar's household, Joseph was falsely accused of sexual harassment by his master's wife, and ended up in prison. It was from his despair in prison that he was elevated to the throne of Egypt. (Genesis 41).

As good as Joseph looked sitting on the throne, none of it had been accomplished by the effecting of a great personal plan.

Our path to destiny often begins with a collision with the rushing river of God's purpose.   That encounter is usually quite unpleasant. Human nature demands that we build a bridge over the river so we can continue walking on the sure ground of our own plans, but the call of God directs us to step in and be swept away.

Abraham stepped in and allowed the river to carry him to *terrae incognitae* in obedience to God's call. It was the same river that cut into Moses' contentment in Midian.   After fleeing from Egypt, he had found refuge in Midian and comfort in the arms of Zipporah, the daughter of Jethro the priest.   He had arrived a stranger and ended up the son-in-law and steward of the riches of the most important man in the land!   The Bible tells us *"Moses was content to dwell with the man."* (Exodus 2:21).

Mary encountered it at a most inconvenient time.   The journey of her life had brought the reward of marriage within reach.   She was betrothed to Joseph, a God-fearing young man of royal stock (Luke 1:27), when God asked her to accept the working of the Spirit in her womb (Luke 1:26-37/Matthew 1:18-21).

For Gideon the encounter came at the threshing floor in Ophrah while he was doing the responsible thing - making sure that his family was provided for during a time of siege.

> *"Go in this thy might,"*

the Lord told him in Judges 6:14,

> *"and thou shalt save Israel from the hand*
> *of the Midianites: have not I sent thee?"*

What might?   God was talking to the wrong man.   With what was he supposed to save Israel?   Besides, there were more urgent things to attend to.   He had to finish threshing and hiding the wheat before the marauding Midianites arrived.

Choosing the faith road is never easy.   Our way often seems more responsible than God's.   In the end, we settle on being "good" and "responsible" Christians who are proficient at threshing and hiding the wheat from the Midianites, instead of allowing ourselves to be empowered to destroy the enemy.

God interrupts our lives to bring us into the stream of His power, and to line us up with His purpose. Proverbs 19:21 tells us that the plans in a man's heart are many, but ultimately it's the Lord's purpose that will prevail. He interrupts our lives to invite us to what He is committed to, and when we accept the invitation and walk in His will, He prospers our way.

We miss the blessing of His purpose when we dismiss the worth of the detour because of the rudeness of the invitation. Paul became one of the greatest Christian leaders of all time after being struck by a lightning bolt from heaven that left him blind for three days (Acts 9:1-9). It is easy to think that he deserved a rude invitation because he was a determined murderer who needed to encounter the reality of a jealous and powerful God.

We are no less set in lifestyles that don't please God than Paul was, and have as much need to encounter the reality of a jealous and powerful God as he did. Our generation's roots are sunk too deep in the culture of the fall to hear a gentle call, or to respond to a gentle nudging. We have drunk from the cup of the harlot, and are in a slumber too deep to wake from a whisper. Because of the lateness of the hour and the intensity of the battle, the important thing is not how He calls us but that we respond.

the CHALLENGE - > Can God change your plans?

1. What personal circumstances would make it challenging for you to radically change course?

2. Obedience often takes us into unfamiliar territory. How does your faith help you deal with being in an unfamiliar place?

3. Does God always require us to abandon our plans to follow His, or is it acceptable to try and find common ground between our plans and His?

Personal lessons learned from Chapter I

1.
2.
3.

"There is a way which seemeth right unto a man, but the end thereof are the ways of death."
- Proverbs 14:12

Here Am I, Send Me!

Whom shall I send,
and who will go for Us?

ISAIAH 6:8

Isaiah's confession of
availability was made
in a state of drunkenness
induced by God's glory.

Any serious student of theology will tell you that God is perfectly capable of achieving His goals without us. Yet there is an underlying tone of desperation in these words.

"Whom shall I send, and who will go for Us?"

It sounds almost blasphemous to suggest that God needs us, and needs us desperately. In Luke 19:40 Jesus exploded the myth of man's indispensability to God. After some Pharisees had complained about the disciples rejoicing and praising God with a loud voice He answered them:

> *"I tell you that, if these should hold their peace, the stones would immediately cry out."*

If He can cause rocks to sing His praises and transform donkeys into prophets, then there is a reason other than our indispensability why He needs us.

God does not call us out of lack on His part. Because He is God, He lacks nothing. He could have liberated the children of Israel without Moses and defended them from the Midianites without Gideon, but He chose to do it through them. He does not need prophets to be heard. He does not use any of us because He cannot do without us, but because He chooses to.

What an awesome thing it is to be needed by God! We witness in Isaiah 6 a great God choosing to need a frail man who cannot abide His presence. God expresses His need to Isaiah in the form of a question, and not a command:

> *"Whom shall I send, and who will go for Us?"*

It was up to Isaiah to respond. Only a few moments before, Isaiah's wretchedness had been revealed in the brightness of God's glory, prompting Isaiah to cry out in fear (verse 5):

> *"Woe is me! for I am undone; because I am a man of unclean lips, and I dwell in the midst of a people of unclean lips; for mine eyes have seen the King, the Lord of hosts".*

But God would not allow Isaiah to dwell in a paralyzing awareness of his wretchedness. He quickly dispatched an angel to respond to Isaiah's fear and self-condemnation. Touching his lips with a live coal, the angel declared:

"thine iniquity is taken away, and thy sin purged."

Surely the great God Jehovah, Maker of heaven and earth was entitled to command His creation to serve Him! Yet He neither commanded nor condemned Isaiah. Instead He cleansed him and gave him the choice to respond.

Two things were revealed to Isaiah by this experience: the greatness of God and the greatness of His love. He understood that responding to God's need was honoring His desire. We can almost hear the humbled prophet choking as he responds to God's desperation:

"Here am I; send me" (verse 8).

Isaiah understood from this experience that availability is a function of choice, and that God expects us to draw His attention to our availability. It was only after He had sent a clear message to God that he was available that God sent him.

A study of the Scriptures also shows that availability leads to more communion with God. Had Isaiah not been available, the story of his experience with the Lord would most likely have ended in Isaiah 6. We have sixty more chapters beyond the glorious encounter in the temple because Isaiah said yes in chapter 6. God reveals more of Himself, His plans and purposes to those who are available to Him.

Moses would not have had any further revelatory conversations and encounters with God if he had insisted that he was not available for the mission to deliver the children of Israel. It would not have been necessary for God to continue showing him His ways.

God continued talking to Paul after his Damascus Road conversion because he was available. We cannot expect an extension of a revelatory relationship with God when we are not available to be sent by Him.

Isaiah also understood that God was not asking him for suggestions about who to send. He had not revealed Himself to Isaiah in this glorious way so He could hear Isaiah's suggestions. Recognizing that, Isaiah made sure that he spoke for himself, that he confessed his own availability and not someone else's.

God often hears our suggestions when what we need to offer Him is our availability. We offer our suggestions so we can avoid taking the detour, and continue in our way.   We tell God that He would be better off calling others who earn less money than we do. We tell Him the kingdom is better off with us pursuing our careers so we can be a financial blessing to the work of ministry, suggesting by our response that He needs our money more than our obedience.

Isaiah knew it was not up to him to decide how he would serve God. He would not demand to know the details of the assignment before deciding on his availability. What mattered was not the nature of the assignment, but the fact that it was God who was calling. He would not make God wait for his answer while he went on an endless round of consultations with friends and family before deciding. He would not risk having someone dissuade him from doing what he knew he needed to do. Who knew better than Isaiah the reality of what he had experienced? To whom had the glory of God been revealed? This was a decision for Isaiah, and him alone.

Like Isaiah, Paul knew that there were some decisions only the person who had gone through a particular experience could make. He writes in Galatians 1:15-17:

> *"…when it pleased God, who separated me from my mother's*

womb, and called me by his grace, to reveal His Son in me, that I might preach Him among the heathen; immediately I conferred not with flesh and blood: Neither went I up to Jerusalem to them which were apostles before me; but I went into Arabia, and returned again unto Damascus".

He conferred not with flesh and blood because his experience did not need validation through consultation. He refused to subject his availability to the opinions of those who had not experienced what he had.

Isaiah also understood the importance of making the decision while the experience was still fresh, just as Moses had needed to make his decision in the mountain before encountering his great father-in-law and looking into the beautiful eyes of the Midianite woman that he loved. Those who exit their experience with God without making the decisions called for by that experience often find it difficult to make the decisions afterwards. Some decisions can only be made "under the influence". They become harder to make once we come down the mountain. Isaiah's confession of availability was a clear case of *deciding under the influence.* It was made in a state of drunkenness induced by God's glory.

Notice the two parts to Isaiah's confession of availability: He announces first that he is in position:

"Here am I;"

Secondly, he makes the purpose for which he is available clear:

"Send me".

Isaiah was in a position to be sent. Are you in a position to be sent?

We must be careful where we sink our roots, making sure they are positions from which God can send us. The decisions that we make concerning where we fellowship must position us to be sent by God. Our choices of spouses must send unequivocal messages to God that we are available to be sent.

In 1 Kings 19:19-21, Elisha knew that he had to reposition himself to be sent by God. After the prophet Elijah had cast his mantle upon him, Elisha took the oxen with which he had been ploughing the fields and slew them, boiled their flesh and gave the meat to the people to eat.

> *"Then he arose, and went after Elijah, and ministered unto him".*

He recognized that Abel-meholah was not the place from where God would launch his prophetic ministry. There is no reason to believe that he did not like Abel-meholah. Judging by the number of oxen he was using to plough the fields when Elijah found him, Elisha's family had prospered in that city.

Your Abel-meholah may look like a place of great promise, a prosperous place, an ideal place in your eyes for God to launch you from. The question is, is that where God is? Isaiah said, *Here am I.* He was where God was. God could launch him from where he was. It may not be easy to uproot yourself from where you are. Yet to lay hold of His destiny for your life, you must do whatever it takes to send Him the unequivocal message that Isaiah sent:

Here am I, Send me!

the CHALLENGE - > Can you be sent?

1. If God is perfectly capable of achieving His goals without us, why does He call us?

2. Read Exodus 3. If you were in Moses' shoes, would you have felt that the Lord had given you enough information to convince you to respond to the call?

3. Isaiah volunteered himself in Isaiah 6:8 even though the call was not specifically addressed to Him. Would it have been a sin if he had not?

Personal lessons learned from Chapter 2

1.

2.

3.

...I say to this man, Go, and he goeth; and to another, Come, and he cometh; and to my servant, Do this, and he doeth it
- Matthew 8:9

THREE

Is There Not
A Cause?

Arise; for this matter
belongeth unto thee:
we also will be with thee:
be of good courage,
and do it.

EZRA 10:4

To David, the taunts of the Philistine
and his defiance of the armies
of the living God
were a call to leadership.

Let's journey back to the valley of Elah almost three thousand years ago. Two mortal enemies are arrayed against each other. On one side are the armies of the Philistines, confident and ready to fight, led by the nine-foot behemoth called Goliath. On the other are the terrified armies of Israel with the troubled King Saul at their head.

For forty days and nights, Goliath hurls insults at the armies of Israel, challenging them to produce a leader. For forty days and nights, Israel fails to meet the challenge.

A young shepherd boy by the name of David arrives on the scene and witnesses the pride of the giant and the terror of his people. As he talks with his brothers who are soldiers in the army of Israel, the giant emerges to mock Israel as he has been doing for the past forty days (1 Samuel 17:23), prompting the men of Israel to flee in terror.

David is disturbed by the response of Israel's warriors, and says as much, provoking a sharp rebuke from his oldest brother Eliab:

> *"...and Eliab's anger was kindled against David, and he said, Why camest thou down hither? and with whom hast thou left those few sheep in the wilderness? I know thy pride, and the naughtiness of thine heart; for thou art come down that thou mightest see the battle."* (1 Samuel 17:28).

Eliab was angry with David because the young man's presence and questions exposed his own weakness. As the older brother, he knew of David's extraordinary exploits: how he had killed both a lion and a bear with his bare hands. Instead of spouting patronizing and jealous vitriol, should he not have been the one using the words of Shechaniah who told Ezra in Ezra 10:4:

> *"Arise; for this matter belongeth unto thee; we also will be with thee: be of good courage and do it."*

David was not in the least intimidated by his brother's insecurity, responding in the 29th verse of 1 Samuel 17:

> *"What have I now done? Is there not a cause?"*

After responding to Eliab, we read in the 30th verse that he turned away from his brother to talk to someone who had better sense.

Our ability to turn away from our "Eliabs" is critical to the fulfillment of our destinies. David took the keys to his destiny from his brother's grasp by turning away. He refused to be drawn into a pointless argument when there was a more important issue at hand that needed his attention. He had the emotional strength to make his brother know that he would not allow him to stand in the way of his destiny. His refusal to be patronized on account of his age was critical to the success of his mission (1 Timothy 4:12 and Titus 2:15).

David refused to be intimidated by Eliab playing the seniority card because he knew he had the better hand. Once he had put his brother in his place, he pulled out the testimony card, stepped forward and felled the giant.

It is important to note that at no point did David hear a voice from God telling him to go against Goliath. What he heard was the call of the cause. We can never hear the call of the cause if we cannot see that the way things are is not what they are supposed to be. David knew that it was not Israel that was supposed to be afraid. It was not Saul's army that was supposed to be ducking and hiding. They needed to remember God's promise at Kadesh-Barnea that He would put the dread of Israel upon the nations that were *"under the whole heaven"* (Deuteronomy 2:25).

The mere mention of the name *Israel* was supposed to put terror into the hearts of her enemies. According to Rahab's confession to the two spies Joshua sent to Jericho to view the land (Joshua 2:9-11), it was clear God had kept His promise to put the dread of Israel upon the nations. The people of Jericho and the other inhabitants of the land had lived in terror of Israel since they had heard the news of the Lord's mighty deliverance at the Red Sea and Israel's victories against the kings of the Amorites. Upon arriving at Jericho, Joshua and the people of Israel had found the city shut up because of their formidable testimony:

> *"Now Jericho was straitly shut up because of the children of Israel: none went out, and none came in"* (Joshua 6:1-2).

At one time, Israel had even acknowledged that God had kept His promise, singing along with Moses in Exodus 15:13-16:

> *"Thou in Thy mercy hast led forth the people which Thou hast redeemed. Thou hast guided them in thy strength unto thy holy habitation. The people shall hear, and be afraid: sorrow shall take hold on the inhabitants of Palestina…all the inhabitants of Canaan shall melt away. Fear and dread shall fall upon them…"*

There was something terribly wrong with the picture David saw in the valley of Elah. It seemed Israel had forgotten both God's promise to them and their position in His plan.

Since Goliath was challenging not just Israel but the kingdom of God itself, anyone going against Goliath in faith could not fail. David could not fail. He could count on the God who had been his helper in previous battles to help him in what was clearly a kingdom matter:

> *"The Lord that delivered me out of the paw of the lion, and out of the paw of the bear, He will deliver me out of the hand of this Philistine"* (1 Samuel 17:37).

David's success against the giant demonstrates the power of effective testimony deployment. David knew how to use past miracles to address a present challenge. He understood that the value of a miracle was not just the meeting of a present need, but giving those who experience it faith for the future. In Mark 6, shortly after witnessing the powerful miracle of the feeding of the five thousand, Jesus' disciples had encountered a violent storm as they crossed the sea of Galilee in a ship. Noticing them struggling against the storm from the shore where He had remained, Jesus walked on water and entered the ship whereupon the wind ceased. The disciples were astonished, *"amazed in themselves beyond measure, and wondered"* (verse 51). The next verse tells us why they wondered:

> *"For they considered not the miracle of the loaves; for their heart was hardened"* (verse 52).

They could not believe what they had just witnessed. Yet was this not the same Jesus who just hours earlier had worked another astonishing miracle? While there is nothing wrong with being awed by the Lord's ability to work new miracles, it is dangerous when the awe originates from the kind of unbelief that makes us unable to apply our testimony to the present distress.

David knew that in addition to past testimonies being relevant to present and future challenges, they could also be applied to bigger present needs. What Israel faced in the valley of Elah was neither a lion nor a bear, but a whole army. Yet David still went to battle on the strength of his victory against the lion and the bear (1 Samuel 17: 34-37).

Confident in the power of his testimony, he was as proactive in the bigger battle as he had been in the smaller, going after Goliath just as he had gone after the lion and the bear to grab the sheep out of their mouths.

There is risk associated with responding to the call of any cause. David was not acting out of presumptous recklessness, but out of understanding, knowledge and faith.   He understood God's big picture, knew who he was in it, and had faith in God's ability and willingness to help him.

Lack of understanding, knowledge and faith compromises our ability to take risks in response to the call of the cause.   It makes us unable to recognize the purpose of our strategic placement, and diminishes our leadership value.

Queen Esther's leadership value to the Hebrew exiles was diminished by a lack of understanding of what God could do through her. When Mordecai asked her to intercede on behalf of the Jews who were facing the threat of genocide, she was afraid to go to her husband the king because:

> *"...all the king's servants, and the people of the king's provinces, do know, that whosoever, whether man or woman, shall come unto the king into the inner court, who is not called, there is one law of his to put him to death, except such to whom the king shall hold out the golden scepter, that he may live."*
> (Esther 4:11)

What reason did Esther have to be afraid? Why would the king not hold out the golden scepter to his beloved queen? She was neither one of the servants nor a simple subject. Although she was a Jew, she was the apple of the Babylonian king's eye, the one woman he loved above all women in his kingdom.

What risk was she being asked to take here? The risk was only in her mind. This was a cause with Esther's name written all over it. No one else was in a position to do what she was being asked to do. She was the Jew in the palace strategically placed there by God for a bigger reason than simply meeting King Ahasuerus' conjugal needs.

Once Mordecai had challenged her (*"who knoweth whether thou art come to the kingdom for such a time as this?"* Esther 4:14), and she had the necessary understanding, knowledge and faith, she rose to the occasion, and her intercession on behalf of the Jews saved them from extermination.

Deborah the prophetess and judge of Israel (Judges 4) knew that leading the armies of Israel to war against Cisera, as risky as it was, was a more pressing need than cooking her husband Lapidoth's meal. As a mother and wife, she could have conveniently sought to excuse herself from the risky responsibilities of high office. Yet she chose to respond to the risky call of a risky cause to ensure the safety of the people of Israel, including her husband.

In our time, the call of the cause of righteousness shall be louder and more insistent than any other call. It shall give God pleasure when we respond to it as Phinehas the son of Eleazar did in Numbers 25. When one of the men of Israel brought a Midianitish woman into the camp and took her into his tent to lie with her, even as the children of Israel were weeping before the door of the tabernacle asking for God's forgiveness for committing whoredom with the daughters of Moab, Phinehas was incensed. He took a javelin, followed the man and the woman into the tent and killed them.

God was very pleased with Phinehas for turning away His wrath from the children of Israel, and rewarded him with His covenant of peace:

> *"Behold, I give unto him my covenant of peace: And he shall have it, and his seed after him, even the covenant of an everlasting priesthood: because he was zealous for his God, and made an atonement for the children of Israel"*
> (Numbers 25:12-13)

Phinehas took this affront personally. He did not wait to gauge the popular mood before acting. Like David in the valley of Elah, he did not hear a voice from heaven instructing him to kill the offenders. He did not need to go on a long fast before acting. He knew the difference between right and wrong, and he had no choice but to respond to a call that was as loud as it was clear.

Is there not a cause?

the CHALLENGE - > Find your cause

1. How do relationships affect our ability to respond to the causes of our time?

2. Why was David uniquely ready to respond to the challenge of Goliath?

3. Why was God pleased with Phinehas in Numbers 25:12-13?

Personal lessons learned from Chapter 3

1.

2.

3.

Who knoweth whether thou art come to the kingdom for such a time as this?
- Esther 4:14

FOUR

When Duty Calls

And Deborah arose,
and went with Barak to Kedesh.

JUDGES 4:9

The call of duty
is not a demand for payment
for what we got from God,
but fulfilling the responsibility
of what we have become
through His grace.

The welfare reform debate has over the years highlighted a troubling relationship between government handouts and a diminished sense of responsibility in welfare communities. Even the most ardent supporters of social welfare have a difficult time refuting the argument that the welfare system undercuts the development of civic responsibility, and contributes to the victimization of the poor.

While the idea of generosity as an agent for victimization may be difficult to accept, the evidence is abundant particularly in the inner cities of America that the "blessings" of welfare have made many of its beneficiaries more proficient terrors unto themselves and others.

Part of the difficulty of developing a sense of responsibility comes from the inability to attach the right value to things that are freely given. We see the same problem in the word of God with those who have been the recipients of God's extravagant but free favor.

God's grace never came to the children of Israel with a price written on it. As a result, they placed more value on the garlic and leeks of Egypt than on what God had done for them (Numbers 11). When we do not know the value of what was given to us, we fail to develop the sensitivity to respond to the call of civic or kingdom duty.

According to the words of Jesus in Luke 12:48:

> *"...unto whomsoever much is given, of him shall be much required..."*

Those who do not know that they have been given much will exempt themselves from the requirement to respond to the call of duty.

There are some who have a difficulty with the suggestion that God would require anything in return for extending His grace to us since that would imply purchasing what God Himself says is freely given (Matthew 10:8, Romans 3:24, Romans 8:32, 1 Corinthians 2:12).

What Jesus was talking about here was not paying for God's grace anymore than the things we do for our spouses would be considered payment for their love.

The call of kingdom duty is not a demand for payment, but a reminder for us to fulfill the responsibility for what we have become through His grace. It is a call for us to fulfill the responsibility of sonship. When we come into the kingdom we receive the spirit of adoption (Romans 8:15) and become His children *"and if children, then heirs; heirs of God, and joint-heirs with Christ"* (Romans 8:17).

When we do not respond to the call of kingdom duty, we are telling God we are not His children. When we run away from the responsibilities of sonship, we merely confirm to Him that we don't believe we were ever enriched by the blessing of His grace.

While I would not necessarily expect a teenage visitor to my home to take out the trash, my expectations would change if that visitor became my son through adoption. He would take out the trash not as payment for adoption, but because of the blessing of being accepted as a son.

Deborah the judge of Israel (Judges 4) knew that she had been enriched by the blessings of God's grace, as did Lapidoth her husband. When the call of duty came, she knew to go, and he knew to step out of the way. When the children of Israel had cried out to the Lord for deliverance from the oppression of Jabin king of Canaan, she had sent for Barak, the commander of Israel's army and said:

> *"...Hath not the Lord God of Israel commanded saying,*
> *Go and draw toward mount Tabor, and take with thee*
> *ten thousand men of the children of Naphtali and of the*
> *children of Zebulun? And I will draw unto thee to the*
> *river Kishon Sisera, the captain of Jabin's army, with his*
> *chariots and his multitude; and I will deliver him into thine*
> *hand..."* (Judges 4:6-7).

When Barak refused to go without her, Deborah heard the unmistakable call of duty, and rose and went with Barak to Kedesh. Lapidoth got out of the way because he understood that much is required of those to whom much is given. He had been given much, an anointed woman of God and judge of Israel as his wife and all the benefits that came with being married to a person of high rank.

The call of duty can be difficult to respond to without rocking the family boat. Consider the case of Joseph and Mary. According to Matthew 1:18-19,

> "... When as his mother Mary was espoused to Joseph, before they came together, she was found with child of the Holy Ghost. Then Joseph her husband, being a just man, and not willing to make her a publick example, was minded to put her away privily."

Joseph was clearly very disappointed. Who would not have been shaken to discover that the woman to whom they were engaged was carrying someone else's child? It says much about Joseph that he was not willing to humiliate her, but was going to put her away privately. Remarkably, once an angel of the Lord appeared to him in a dream confirming that what was conceived in Mary was of the Holy Ghost and urging him not to put her away, Joseph obeyed.

Not only did he not put her away, but according to the 25th verse he *"...knew her not till she had brought forth her firstborn son: and he called his name JESUS."*

He denied himself what was rightfully his to honor what God was doing in his spouse's life. He denied himself to preserve the purity of her response to the call of duty. He understood that what was his belonged to God first. Because he was a God-fearing man, he would not allow her response to the call to sink the family boat.

It is not always the gravity of the call involved that sinks some marriages. Some boats sink even in calm waters. Those who are yet to marry owe it to themselves to believe God for the kind of spouses who will fear Him enough not to stand in the way of their response to the call.

The river of God's purpose is not a smooth ride even for the best of marriages. It is easy to think we are sinking when we are in it, even when all we are experiencing is the turbulence of progressive motion. The choice that we have is between the motionless and ineffective stability of remaining parked in the garage, or the dynamic and effective unsettledness that comes with seeking to please God and to accomplish His purpose. Joseph and Mary chose the latter, convinced that their marriage would survive their tour of duty.

It would not have survived if they had not had common beliefs. Thankfully, they not only believed in the same God, but also understood His language and the experiences through which He made His will known. As a result, Joseph did not wake up from his dream and dismiss it as just another dream. He knew that it was a visitation from the Lord, just as Mary had known the significance of her encounter with the angel (see Luke 1:26-38). Without that shared understanding of who God was and how He worked, their marriage would have most likely not survived.

The idea of the call of duty suggests an obligatory rather than an elective response. While the Lord does not force us to respond to anything, we must respond to the legitimate causes He opens our eyes to as if we have an obligation to respond. In essence, what distinguishes kingdom leadership from all other forms of leadership is this very idea of voluntary obligation.

In God's kingdom it is the idea of voluntary obligation that aligns duty and passion, engaging the heart with the mechanics of duty. We volunteer because we are believers, and report for duty because we have an obligation to fulfill. When we combine a sense of duty with the passion of believing, we give our response to the call of the cause a cutting edge.

the CHALLENGE - > Discover the joy of duty

1. How difficult is it to respond with a sense of duty to a situation you are not responsible for creating, and from whose resolution you stand to gain nothing?

2. How does attaching the right value to your experience with God help in responding to the call of kingdom duty?

Personal lessons learned from Chapter 4

1.

2.

3.

Unto whomsoever much is given, of him shall be much required.
- Luke 12:48

Move My Heart, O God!

*...and his soul was grieved
for the misery of Israel.*

JUDGES 10:16

*Jesus wept, not because
Israel recognized the state
she was in, but precisely
because she did not.*

We cannot respond to the call of the causes of our time without our hearts being engaged. The forces of post-modernism conspire daily to produce a spiritually blind and self-centered generation that operates with androidal emotional detachment and mostly bases its responses on cold calculations of cost and benefit.

It was that emotional detachment that caused many to be largely unmoved by the 100 day massacre of over 800,000 Tutsis and politically moderate Hutus by the majority Hutu tribe in the Rwanda genocide of 1994. It is that same detachment that today allows international pedophiles from the rich countries of Western Europe and North America to take advantage of lax law enforcement in the emerging democracies of Eastern Europe to sexually exploit innocent children while the rest of the world goes about its business.

We want to pretend that it will take democracy rather than the truth of God's word to resolve the deepening crisis of values, and the application of business management skills to keep the Christian movement afloat. As we try to outdo Satan with our business models, he is building a constituency of believers, going for the vulnerable hearts of the young and raising a generation that not only despises God, but whose very religion is tolerance, acceptance and promotion of everything that is an abomination to God. We will invariably lose the war when our only defense against the advance of the kingdom of darkness is a Christian technocracy.

Satan's work is to ensure that we are either too blind to see, or too emotionally inured to be engaged. When we are troubled by the way things are, he makes sure that like Lot, we are not troubled enough to act. 2 Peter 2: 7-8 tells us that Lot was *vexed with the filthy conversation of the wicked: (for that righteous man dwelling among them, in seeing and hearing, vexed his righteous soul from day to day with their unlawful deeds)*. He was "troubled" yet content to dwell in Sodom, "troubled", but not enough to be moved.

After the angels warned him to leave Sodom to escape the judgment, we read in Genesis 19:16 that Lot hesitated:

> *"And while he lingered, the men laid hold upon his*
> *hand, and upon the hand of his wife, and upon the hand*
> *of his two daughters; the LORD being merciful unto*
> *him: and they brought him forth, and set him without the city."*

Why did he linger? He lingered because he considered it his home and place of business, not his mission. He had chosen this place for himself after parting ways with Abraham following their servants' dispute over pastures in Genesis 13. He lingered not out of a desire to bring righteousness to Sodom, but because he considered Sodom a "good" place for his investment portfolio. It was a "great" place to live, with its picturesque view of the Edenic and well-watered plains of Jordan (Genesis 13:10-11). Little wonder that his wife could not resist one last wistful look, despite the warning from the angels that no one was to look back at the Lord's destruction of Sodom and Gomorrah and the verdant beauty of the plains.

We sink our roots so deep into the business of living that we are not easily moved even when the call of the cause is loud and clear. When the causes of the kingdom compete for our heart's attention with the business of living, the latter invariably wins. Jesus makes it clear in Luke 12:24-34 that we cannot free our hearts to be moved by the things that move God's heart without surrendering the business of living to His providential care:

> *"For where your treasure is, there will your heart be also"* (verse 34).

The heart of the rich young man in Matthew 19 could not be pried away from his earthly treasure to be responsive to God's causes. We contradict ourselves when we ask God to give us sensitivity to kingdom causes while resisting His efforts to separate our hearts from the things that inure us to the cries of the lost and the hopelessness of humanity.

It is not just the business of life that is responsible for the death of sensitivity. The business of ministry has been just as much a culprit, with the emergence of the CEO pastor whose responsibility is to the bottom line, and whose success is largely measured by the number of drive-through services conducted in one day. Many churches today are models of efficiency and organization resulting from cutting out the "waste" of involvement, relationship, and practical compassion. Like the Priest and the Levite of Luke 10:31-32, we charge past the wounded to fulfill our ministry engagements, finding it beneath us to stoop to raise the weary and to commit precious time to the need that disrupts the program.

What God is looking for are those who, like the Good Samaritan, will have time to see the need. Coming upon the wounded man, he

"...saw him, (and)...had compassion on him" (Luke 10:33).

It is not possible to have compassion on what we cannot see. Our hearts cannot be moved if we cannot see. The pace dictated by the business mindset often causes us to outrun the needs and to be unable to focus on what God wants us to see.

By its very nature, Godly compassion is disruptive, forcing generosity of time and resources in violation of the carefulness of business. God is impressed not so much by our ability to accomplish great projects, but by our ability to show His mercy. Admonishing us to follow the example of the Samaritan, Jesus' message to us is clear:

"...Go and do likewise."

A few years ago, during a ministry trip to the capital of an African country, I found my car surrounded by a group of homeless street children, each one loudly pressing his case to guard the car for some change while I went into a bank. Encountering children in similar circumstances years before had troubled me enough to weep for the sins of a country that allowed the lives of their children to be wasted away on the streets. This time around however, I was too busy to care and extremely irritated by their aggressive and arrogant soliciting methods. I wondered to myself why the government did not just round all of them up and put them in juvenile detention centers!

The problem had not changed. It was my heart which had. Seeking to rationalize the hardness of my own heart, I told myself that some of the kids seemed to be enjoying their life on the street. Why should I be troubled if they did not seem to be troubled by their own situation?

One of the devil's most effective weapons is convincing those who need help that they don't, hence the cocaine addict who threatens to do violence to those seeking to help, and the anger of the dysfunctional inner-city mother towards those who dare to teach her self-control. Still, the hardness of their hearts is no justification for the hardening of our own.

In Luke 19:41-44, Jesus wept for Jerusalem, not because she recognized how fallen she was. He wept precisely because she did not. He wept over her blindness, her inability to see *the things which belong unto (her) peace!*" He wept because she did not know the day of her visitation.

It was not Jesus who was blind and had gone off course. It was not Him who was going to suffer the consequences of disobedience. Yet it was Jesus doing the weeping even as Israel persisted in sin.

Our hearts must be moved neither by the popularity of the cause, nor the enthusiasm of those who would benefit from it, but by the fact that it is right. Had Lot recognized that Sodom was ripe for evangelism and began to preach repentance, he might have been the only one preaching, but that would not have made him wrong.

In Ezra 10:1, Ezra cast himself down in the house of God, weeping and confessing Israel's sin, not because it was the popular thing to do, but because it was right. When the others saw it, they too gathered. Men, women and children were found weeping and confessing their sins. They took their cue from Ezra. There is always the risk that when we are the first ones to be moved, others will not immediately follow. We may have to bear the emotional burden for responding to kingdom causes by ourselves for longer than we would like. It may take longer for us to have companions in the cause willing to shoulder the responsibilities associated with leadership. That would still not make the cause wrong.

We must guard against the diminishing of our ability to respond with compassion as our station in life improves. We must not lose the ability to weep for those in distress as we climb up the social ladder. In the book of Esther, Mordecai would not allow Esther to get away with her indifference to the plight of the Jews simply because the former slave had become queen in the land of captivity.

In Nehemiah 1:1-4 we read about another Hebrew serving in a less exalted position in the court of King Artaxerxes. For a slave, being the king's cupbearer was still a position of considerable privilege and influence. Informed by visitors from Jerusalem of the affliction of the remnant and the dilapidated state of the walls of the city of God, Nehemiah was not just touched enough to weep, but to intercede for Israel both with God and with King Artaxerxes. He was troubled enough to acquire a sense of mission.

The extent to which our hearts can be moved reveals the depth of our love for the things that are important to God. Nehemiah's tears revealed the depth of his love for Israel. It was not just the state of his personal house that was important to him, but the state of God's people.

I have very vivid memories of the first funeral I attended as a child. With no understanding of the meaning of death, I was bewildered by the sight of my father, uncles, mother and aunts weeping uncontrollably. I started crying because everyone was crying, and because it seemed the right thing to do. Running out of tears after several minutes and realizing I could not keep up with the adults, I started looking around, trying to attract the attention of the other kids so we could go outside to play.

Finding no takers and getting a clear message from the stern look of a male relative who was sitting across from me that this was not a time to play but to mourn, I took a deep breath and let out a hyenic howl, which startled everyone including myself, and raised the mourning to another level. Several relatives mourned for several days thereafter, even when the sun seemed to shine again and the children had returned to play.

I understood clearly from the depth of the grief of the adults the extent of their connectedness to the deceased. What they had, which I lacked, was a deeper sense of what we had lost.

Much as we may not like those who sternly remind us that this is not the time for play, that does not change the truth that God is looking to reinstate the weeping leader who has the sensitivity to be broken by the misery of God's people. He seeks to raise those whose hearts can be moved with the same depth of emotion as the servants of God of old.

In 2 Kings 8:11, we read that *"the man of God* (Elisha) *wept"*. He wept because he could see what was going to come upon Israel when Hazael ascended the throne of Syria. He wept for the innocents - the children Hazael would dash, and the pregnant women whose bellies he would rip with the sword.

What is impressive to God is not so much the tears that we shed, but the heart they reveal. For the leaders of old, weeping was not the end but the beginning. They were moved to intercession and to mission. God is not pleased with mere sensitivity but also with what we do about what we see.

Our brokenness moves God's heart. It was the brokenness of Lazarus' sisters, friends and relatives that moved Jesus' heart in John 11:33-36. What option did Jesus have after being so touched except to resurrect Lazarus? What else can Jesus do after being touched by the brokenness of leaders except to resurrect the church?

the CHALLENGE - > **What moves your heart?**

1. Does your faith make you more responsive to the needs of others? What do you measure your responsiveness by?

2. To what extent should our compassion depend on the value those we try to help place on it?

3. What lesson do we learn from the Good Samaritan about balancing our compassion with the need to be about our other business?

Personal lessons learned from Chapter 5

1.

2.

3.

For where your treasure is, there will your heart be also
- Luke 12:34.

SIX

Wherewith Shall I Save Israel?

*Behold my family is
poor in Manasseh,
and I am the least
in my father's house.*

JUDGES 6:15

*The key to Israel's victories
over her enemies was the
Emmanuel Factor.*

When the angel spoke to Gideon in Judges 6 charging him to save Israel from the hand of the Midianites, Gideon immediately made it known that he was resource-challenged.

"wherewith shall I save Israel?"

In addition to being deficient in material resources, he was poor in the testimony department, having never distinguished himself with any heroic exploits against man or beast.

Many would have found the Lord's response to Gideon less than reassuring. Instead of detailing the resources He was going to make available to him for this difficult mission, the Lord said:

> "*...I will be with thee*" (verse 16).

In the Biblical leadership model, the one thing God guarantees those who respond to His call is His presence. Since the Lord's presence is not a quantifiable, tangible resource which we can factor into a business plan or feasibility study, it is often not the answer that we want when we cry out for resources.

His presence was God's promise to Jacob in Genesis 28:15 as he navigated the rugged circumstances of his life journey:

> *"And, behold, I am with thee, and will keep thee in all places whither thou goest, and will bring thee again into this land; for I will not leave thee, until I have done that which I have spoken to thee of."*

Moses understood the importance of God's presence and was convinced that without it, his mission was doomed to fail. Fearful that the Lord would abandon the children of Israel because of their sin, he cried to God at Mt. Sinai:

> *"If thy presence go not with me, carry us not up hence"*
> (Exodus 33:15).

After sinning with Bath-sheba, David was distressed at the prospect of being separated from God's presence. He cried in desperation in the 51st Psalm:

> *"Cast me not away from thy presence"* (verse 11).

We cannot tap into the wealth of His presence without understanding its significance to our calls. The prophet Isaiah was convinced that the key to Israel's victories over her enemies was the "Emmanuel Factor." To the congregating armies of the king of Assyria and those with whom they were confederate, he boldly declared in Isaiah 8: 9-10:

> *"Associate yourselves, O ye people, and ye shall be broken in pieces; and give ear, all ye of far countries: gird yourselves, and ye shall be broken in pieces; gird yourselves, and ye shall be broken in pieces. Take counsel together, and it shall come to nought; speak the word, and it shall not stand: for <u>God is with us</u>".*

What would save Israel was not numerical strength nor the best equipment money could buy. It was the presence of the Lord!

In Acts 5:38-39, Gamaliel, a Pharisee and doctor of the law who had understood the lessons of history, warned the disciples' persecutors of the folly of fighting against anything in which God was involved:

> *"And now I say unto you, Refrain from these men, and let them alone: for if this counsel or this work be of men, it will come to nought: But if it be of God, ye cannot overthrow it; lest haply ye be found even to fight against God."*

What God was trying to get through to Gideon in Judges 6 was that His presence was the greatest resource he would ever need to fulfill the call.

Our anxiety about resources betrays a lack of understanding that great exploits in the Scriptures are not a triumph of material resources, but of the presence of God in His purpose. Armed with God's purpose and backed by His presence, anyone could have saved Israel from the hand of the Midianites.

It's important to understand that delivering Israel from the Midianites meant fighting against real people with real weapons (see chapter 15, Leadership by Faith and the Power Annointing). Gideon was being asked not only to go into a "real" war seemingly without resources, but to also believe that the presence of an invisible God was his greatest weapon.

We often play a double game with the fundamental truth concerning the power and reality of the invisible, embracing it when it serves our convenience, and rejecting it when it threatens our sense of control. Interestingly, the dramatic improvement in the quality of life in our time has largely been based on yesterday's "voodoo science" which has given us microwave ovens that cook our food without a visible flame and little electronic boxes with which we can communicate with a rover on the planet Mars millions of miles away. Indeed, today's science was yesterday's magic, and today's scientists yesterday's sorcerers who would have qualified to be burnt at the stake.

In matters of faith, the trend is the reverse. Even as the numbers of those who claim to believe increases, yesterday's faith is increasingly becoming today's superstition, and those who today claim total dependence on the presence of God for the fulfillment of their calls put their credibility on the line. When the only proof of calling that counts is the financing in hand, the tragic consequence is the exclusion from leadership of those who are poor in "resources" but rich in faith. The result is that we can end up building works that are not products of a true testimony of God's doing.

According to Psalm 127:1 we build in vain when the Lord Himself does not build the house. If He is going to build it Himself, then He has to be present. When He does the building, He utilizes what we have a tendency to discard, with marvelous results:

> *"The stone which the builders refused is become the head stone of the corner. This is the Lord's doing; it is marvelous in our eyes"* (Psalm 118:22-23).

When we fail to recognize the value of His presence, we will despair of our lack of resources. Like Asaph, a minister during David's time, we will become envious of the prosperity of the wicked, and sin against God (Psalm 73). At the height of his frustration, Asaph wondered if God was worth serving:

> *"Verily I have cleansed my heart in vain, and washed my hands in innocency."* (verse 13).

In an epiphanic encounter in "the sanctuary of God" (verse 17), the Lord opened Asaph's eyes to the sorry end of the wicked:

> *"Surely thou didst set them in slippery places; thou castedst them down into destruction. How are they brought into desolation, as in a moment! they are utterly consumed with terrors. As a dream when one awaketh; so, O Lord, when thou awakest, thou shalt despise their image"* (verse 17-20).

From this encounter, Asaph understood the firmness of the foundation under those who recognize that God's presence is more important than material resources. He understood that it was God's presence, not resources, that would give him a sure footing for his ministry.

The words of a repentant Asaph contrasted sharply with his earlier ones:

> *"…it is good for me to draw near to God: I have put my trust in the Lord GOD, that I may declare all thy works"* (verse 28).

> *"Thou shalt guide me with thy counsel, and afterward receive me to glory"* (verse 24).

From mourning the sorry state of his resources, the same Asaph began to speak of the Lord as *"…the strength of my heart, and my portion for ever."*

He was echoing David's declaration in Psalm 16:5

> *"The Lord is the portion of mine inheritance and of my cup: thou maintainest my lot."*

God wants us to remove our focus from material resources and to have confidence in His providential management of our calls. David was quite happy with the Lord maintaining his lot and determining the portion of his inheritance. He knew that God would give him what was necessary for his journey, a sufficient portion for his call.

What God was looking for from Gideon was the kind of obedience that would connect him to God's providence, not questions on budget issues. When we say to Him: "Great idea Lord, but where is the money? Where are the resources?" we accuse Him of being a confused and sloppy God who liberally sows the seeds of vision without making adequate provision. We question His commitment to the fulfillment of His prophetic intent. Why would He call us to assignments that He has not provided for?

Gideon's success against the Midianites was guaranteed because of the Lord's presence. If God was going with him, then any discussion of provision was moot. For God to withhold His provision from Gideon would have been to work against Himself.

God knows exactly what we need, and His presence ensures that we don't have too far to run when we are in need. We cannot wish for a better quartermaster than God. The truth of Philippians 4:19 cannot be diminished by the fact that it has become something of a cliché. God does promise, and is well able to supply all our needs according to His riches in glory.

We must be convinced of His commitment to the success of our calls, and that He has no reason to withhold from us that which we need to fulfill His purpose. It is, after all, His purpose that He calls us to fulfill. He makes that point clear to Gideon in the 14th verse of the 6th chapter of Judges:

> "...thou shalt save Israel from the hand of the Midianites: **have not I sent thee?**" (emphasis added).

Gideon was not going on his own mission. He was going on the Lord's. We must respond to the challenge of leadership not because of what we can do through the resources that we have, but because we discern God's prophetic intent and allow Him to fulfill it through us. God's prophetic intent during Gideon's time was to save Israel from the hand of the Midianites. He was so committed to it that He could accomplish it with anyone who was willing. It was not a question of resources, but of obedience.

It is also important to understand that God's care for His servants extends to their daily and personal bread. When we are able to see ourselves as being part of His army, we will soldier on, assured that the Ultimate Quartermaster will supply all our personal needs. Matthew 6 tells us:

"Therefore take no thought, saying, What shall we eat? or, What shall we drink? or, Wherewithal shall we be clothed?...for your heavenly Father knoweth that ye have need of all these things" (verses 31-32).

"Take therefore no thought for the morrow: for the morrow shall take thought for the things of itself..." (verse 34).

His presence not only guarantees provision, but the power to extend the little that we may have in hand. In Judges 7, He enables Gideon's army of three hundred to sound like the host of heaven, and to conquer a coalition of the Amalekites, the Midianites and "all the children of the east" whose troops were

"...like grasshoppers for multitude; and their camels were without number, as the sand by the sea side for multitude" (Judges 7:12.)

In John 6, seeing the distress of the multitude which had been following Him and had gone for a long time without food, Jesus turned to one of His disciples and asked:

"Whence shall we buy bread, that these may eat?" (John 6:5).

Knowing how depleted their purse was, the disciple answered:

"Two hundred pennyworth of bread is not sufficient for them, that everyone of them may take a little" (John 6:7).

Another disciple responded that there was a young boy who had five barley loaves and two small fishes, adding:

"but what are they among so many?"(John 6:9).

The two disciples were not convinced that what was in hand was sufficient to meet the need.

After taking the loaves and the fish from the boy, and giving thanks, Jesus gave them to the disciples to distribute to the people.

What followed was one of the most powerful miracles of resource extension recorded in the Scriptures. The people not only ate their fill, but there were enough leftovers to fill twelve baskets (John 6:13). What was left over was more than what they had started off with.

Wherewith shall we save Israel? Wherewith shall we accomplish the things that God has called us to?

With God.

the CHALLENGE - ⟩ Make Him your all

1. Are the resources God provides us proof of His presence?

2. What does the presence of God in our calls guarantee?

3. Read Psalm 73. What is the most important lesson of this psalm?

Personal lessons learned from Chapter 6

1.

2.

3.

If thy presence go not with me, carry us not up hence.
- Exodus 33:15

SEVEN

Transition

*The greatest leadership
lessons are learnt in solitude.*

*The Lord will often leave us
with nothing more to start with
than the knowledge that He
has called us.*

The prophet Samuel was a man on a mission. Immediately after arriving in Bethlehem, he summoned Jesse and his sons to the sacrifice so he could carry out the Lord's instruction to anoint Israel's next king. Soon after identifying David as the chosen one, the prophet "took the horn of oil, and anointed him in the midst of his brethren..." (1 Samuel 16:13).

Having been anointed king, what was David supposed to do? How does one transition from being a shepherd to a king? The momentous visit from the prophet had not changed the fact that David was still a boy and the youngest of Jesse's sons. He could have used some guidance from the prophet, but after anointing him, Samuel took off for Ramah almost as hastily as he had appeared in Bethlehem (1 Samuel 16:13b).

This was in sharp contrast to the guidance the same prophet had

provided Saul. After a private anointing ceremony, (1 Samuel 9:27-
10:1) the prophet had summoned all of Israel to Mizpeh to a public
inquiry of the Lord concerning who was to be king. Having already
been told by the Lord that Saul was to be king, and after anointing
him, what purpose did the public enquiry serve if not just to facilitate
Saul's acceptance by the people?

After Saul's public selection, Samuel took time to give the people and
their young king instructions on how to run the kingdom, spelling
out in a detailed manual the rights and duties of the king and his
subjects.

A few days after the young king had successfully gone to battle
against the Ammonites, Samuel picked the euphoric moment of
Israel's victory for Saul's official installation (1 Samuel 11:14-15):

> *"Then said Samuel to the people, Come, and let us go to Gilgal,
> and renew the kingdom there. And all the people went to
> Gilgal, and there they made Saul king before the Lord in Gilgal;
> and there they sacrificed sacrifices of peace offerings before the
> Lord; and there Saul and all the men of Israel rejoiced greatly."*

All of Samuel's actions were designed to help Saul's transition to
the throne. David received no such help. No leadership manual
was placed in his hands. There was no public installation ceremony.
Instead the prophet hastily retreated to Ramah.

Samuel had good reason not to hang around David any longer
than was absolutely necessary after anointing him. When God had
commanded him to anoint David, the prophet had made no secret
of his fears:

> *"And Samuel said, How can I go? If Saul hear it,*

he will kill me." (I Samuel 16:2).

Anointing David when Saul was still on the throne was most certainly going to be viewed by the incumbent as an act of treason.

Samuel was not to be the last prophet presented with such a dilemma by God. Displeased with the rule of Ahab the wicked king of Israel several generations later, God instructed the prophet Elijah to anoint Jehu the son of Nimshi to replace Ahab (1 Kings 19:16). Terrified of incurring Ahab's wrath, Elijah never carried out the Lord's instruction, leaving the dangerous responsibility to Elisha his successor (2 Kings 9).

Elijah did have the courage to carry out the less dangerous assignment of anointing his own successor although he was not too keen to mentor him. When Elisha tried to follow after Elijah had anointed him, the prophet would not let him, only relenting when the young man persisted (1 Kings 19:20-21).

Elijah was a weary prophet on the run with very little energy or enthusiasm to spare to train Elisha. Others may simply be too busy fulfilling God's agendas (or their own) to have time to help the next generation of leaders through their transitional challenges.

The newly called often discover that the Lord will leave them with nothing more to start with than the knowledge that He has called them. They feel shortchanged when learning the hard lesson that they must wait in patience on the same God to reveal the details of His purpose for their lives at a time and place of His choosing.

For David the foundation of God's purpose for his life was laid in isolation. Some of the greatest lessons that would guide his leadership were learnt in solitude, in a classroom with the perfect teacher-to-pupil ratio, a class size of one with the Holy Spirit as the teacher. David was never really alone even after Samuel had returned to Ramah. Notice that on the occasion of David's anointing, the Spirit of the Lord immediately came upon him to accompany him on the journey of his call:

> *"...and the Spirit of the LORD came upon David from that day forward".*(1 Samuel 16:13),

While the old prophets may beat a hasty retreat to their hideouts, the newly-called can count on His Spirit for guidance in their transition.

Jesus also faced some difficult challenges of transition. Evidently Joseph and Mary struggled with the challenge of preparing their child for His extraordinary call. Who wouldn't have? How did one train the Messiah? What were they supposed to do beyond raising Him in a home where they faithfully kept the feasts and obeyed the law?

In Luke 2:41-50 the young Jesus took the matter of His preparation into His own hands. Joseph and Mary had brought Him to Jerusalem for the Feast of the Passover, as was their custom. On their way back to Nazareth after the feast, they had traveled a day's journey when they discovered that He was missing. Returning to Jerusalem they found the twelve-year-old in the temple sitting among the men of letters, *"both hearing them, and asking them questions"*, and astonishing everyone present with His understanding and answers. When they expressed their disappointment for the anxiety he had caused them, He responded:

> *"How is it that you sought Me? Wist ye not that I must be about My Father's business?"* (Verse 49).

We don't find much else written about Jesus' preparation between the age of twelve and the beginning of His public ministry at age thirty. The surprise of the people when He started His ministry was most likely because as far as anyone knew, He had received no special training to prepare Him for that role (Matthew 13:54-56):

> *"And when He was come into His own country, He taught them in their synagogue, insomuch that they were astonished, and said, Whence hath this man this wisdom, and these mighty works? Is not this the carpenter's son? Is not His mother called Mary? and His brethren, James, and Joses, and Simon, and Judas? And His sisters, are they not all with us? Whence then hath this man all these things?"*

His preparation had been an inner work of God. Since the process of God's inner work is not readily visible to those around us, it often does little to help them have confidence in us (see the reaction of Jesus' family and friends to His ministry in Mark 3: 21-35).

Jesus knew better than to allow the skepticism of others to stop Him from walking in His calling. He understood that the fulfillment of the father's purpose for His life was not supposed to be dependent on the approval of others, but on His own obedience.

Aspects of Jesus' personal circumstances would have presented problems in any society. An unemployed single man in his thirties going about claiming to be the Son of God was an inviting target for ridicule. It did not help matters that God's choice as the primary promoter of Jesus' ministry was His cousin John, a locust eating, leather-clad and wilderness-dwelling recluse (Matthew 3:1-4).

God's choice of John as the preparer of the way revealed that God is more interested in laying a foundation of truth than of credibility.

This was not a political campaign but a kingdom assignment. Jesus Himself recognized the importance of John's ministry as a foundation for His own. In one of the most astonishing acts of humility recorded in the Scriptures, the Son of God submitted to John's ministry at the river Jordan, triggering God's public confirmation of His own ministry (Matthew 3:16-17):

> *"...and, lo, the heavens were opened unto Him, and He saw the Spirit of God descending like a dove, and lighting upon Him: And lo, a voice from heaven, saying, This is My beloved Son, in Whom I am well pleased".*

God's choice as facilitators for our calls may not be the kind of people we ourselves would choose. They may not look the way we would like them to look. They may not have the kinds of resources we would like them to have. They may not help our credibility with people. Like Jesus however, we must be able to look beyond all that to see God's purpose.

How confident was Jesus in His call? Confident enough to call others to follow Him and to train them to become leaders even though He had never been a leader before:

> *"And He saith unto them, Follow Me, and I will make you fishers of men"* (Matthew 4:19:)

The apostle Paul was equally confident in his ministry despite the fact that after his Damascus road experience, he had not been mentored by the disciples who had more experience than him:

> *"...when it pleased God, who separated me from my mothers womb, and called me by His grace, to reveal His Son in me, that I might preach among the heathen; immediately I conferred*

not with flesh and blood: neither went I up to Jerusalem to them which were apostles before me; but I went into Arabia, and returned again unto Damascus. Then after three years I went up to Jerusalem to see Peter, and abode with him fifteen days. But other of the apostles saw I none, save James the Lord's brother" (Galatians 1:15-19).

Paul was not saying there is no place for human mentoring in the development of our calls. What he was talking about was the importance of allowing God to lay the primary foundation. Besides, the disciples were initially not willing to admit him into their circle. When he had tried to join them after the Jews in Damascus had tried to kill him, they had only accepted him temporarily after Barnabas had interceded on his behalf:

"...he assayed to join himself to the disciples; but they were all afraid of him, and believed not that he was a disciple. But Barnabas took him, and brought him to the apostles, and declared unto them how he had seen the Lord in the way, and that he had spoken to him, and how he had preached boldly at Damascus in the name of Jesus" (Acts 9:26-27).

When soon thereafter some Grecians sought to kill him, the disciples found an excuse to get rid of him. They sent him off to Tarsus, supposedly for his protection, and promptly forgot about him. Paul only came back to Antioch after Barnabas, on his own initiative, went to find him (Acts 11:25-26). Paul had no choice but to depend on God even as David had depended on Him more than on the prophet Samuel, enabling him to stand even after the prophet's death.

We must be satisfied with where God positions us and who He surrounds us with as we begin the journey of leadership. This is an all-too-familiar story: a young and talented leader, feeling that the small and poor fellowship he is part of does not have the resources to launch his great ministry, bids the church goodbye and leaves to join the largest ministry in town. A few months later, frustrated by his inability to be recognized at the larger fellowship, he is calling the people at his old fellowship, complaining about how "closed" big ministries are.

When we find ourselves flailing helplessly in the muddy waters of our own presumption, the responsibility for our disappointment should rest squarely on us and no one else. From the valley of our disillusionment, we often perceive the places of humble beginnings we despised for what God meant them to be: the vehicles through which God's purposes for our lives would be fulfilled. Instead of setting ourselves up to climb the steep mountain of restoration, we must - like Jesus - watch how we begin.

It was important to Him to begin His ministry with the blessing of an open heaven (Matthew 3:16). When He arrived at the Jordan, John was reluctant to baptize Him. John knew who Jesus was. He had been telling his own disciples about the one who was coming after him whose shoes he was not even worthy to untie. John could not believe it when Jesus showed up to be baptized.

While John was determined to honor Jesus, the Lord was even more determined not to allow John to rob Him of what God intended for Him. As far as Jesus was concerned, it was more important to secure the blessing of an open heaven than the recognition that He was greater than John.

Jesus understood that humility was not only the way to God's heart, but also the way up. According to Proverbs 22:4: (The Living Bible):

"True humility and respect for the Lord lead a man to riches, honor and long life".

and James 4:10:

"Humble yourselves in the sight of the Lord, and he shall lift you up".

God does not expect us to be preoccupied with the search for honor, but to humble ourselves in His sight and trust Him to lift us up. According to Psalm 75:6-7:

"...promotion cometh neither from the east, nor from the west, nor from the south. But God is the judge, He putteth down one, and setteth up another".

Choosing humility over the pride of human ambition is exercising the wisdom of God. We must exercise Godly wisdom in the choices that we make as we embark on the journey of leadership. Proverbs 3:35 tell us:

"The wise shall inherit glory: but shame shall be the promotion of fools."

It is also important that we do not begin our leadership journeys at the expense of others. Jesus did not begin His ministry at John's expense. If anything, He started by confirming it.

David did not start at Saul's expense. He selflessly served the king he had been anointed to replace. He was determined not to begin with blood on his hands. As he fled from the tormented king who had turned on him in spite of his selfless service, David passed on several opportunities to kill him. In one instance, (1 Samuel 26), David and Abishai his lieutenant happened upon a sleeping King Saul, whereupon an excited Abishai exclaimed to David:

> *"God hath delivered thine enemy into thine hand this day: now therefore let me smite him, I pray thee, with the spear even to the earth at once, and I will not smite him the second time"* (verse 8).

David's answer was not what Abishai expected:

> *"…who can stretch forth his hand against the LORD's anointed, and be guiltless?"*

The message was clear: to David being guiltless was more important than ascending to the throne of Israel. He would not even refer to Saul as his enemy, choosing instead to call him "the Lord's anointed"! He would have played into Satan's trap had he allowed himself to see Saul as his enemy. Through wisdom, David kept himself blameless.

Even Saul could not help but bless the young man after David had spared him in 1 Samuel 26: 23-25:

> *"The Lord render to every man his righteousness and his faithfulness: for the Lord delivered thee into my hand to day, but I would not stretch forth mine hand against the LORD's anointed…Then Saul said to David, Blessed be thou, my son David: thou shalt both do great things, and also shalt still prevail."*

The way you begin will determine what will happen with the rest of your journey.

Watch how you begin.

the CHALLENGE - > Beginning God's way

1. What is the place of human mentors in providing transition guidance?

2. How does patience help us through the challenges of transition?

3. What do the psalms teach us about David's struggles during his transition from being a shepherd boy to the throne of Israel?

Personal lessons learned from Chapter 7

1.	
2.	
3.	

"Lead me in thy truth, and teach me: for thou art the God of my salvation; on thee do I wait all the day"
- Psalm 25:5

EIGHT

Learning From The Saddle

Those who are unwilling to endure
the humiliation of learning
never become the people
God wants them to be.

God will call us
to unfamiliar tasks
and hand us the reigns.

Our son could hardly sleep that night. My wife and I had bought him a bicycle for his birthday. Unfortunately, it was in kit form and by the time I finished assembling it, it was too dark outside for him to try it out.

He banged on my bedroom door at dawn and announced that he was ready to ride. As I put his helmet on, he looked into my eyes and said:

"Are you going to teach me?"

I told him I was and sat him on the saddle.

"No, Daddy" he protested as he got off. "I want you to teach me. Don't make me sit there because I don't know how".

Some lessons can only be learnt from the saddle. Instead of taking us through theoretical coursework, God will often compel us to assume the position of a rider, to straddle the bicycle of our assignments in order to learn. To do so, we will have to overcome our fears just as my son had to overcome his. Gideon had to overcome his fears to become judge of Israel, just as Moses had to overcome his to lead the nation of Israel out of captivity. Joseph went from a prison cell to the palace and had to learn the lessons of national leadership from the throne.

One of the biggest problems with learning from the saddle is that learners rarely look good on the saddle. Unfortunately, those who are unwilling to endure the humiliation of learning never become the people God wants them to be. One of my cousins died in his late thirties never having enjoyed the pleasure of riding a bicycle, his desire to ride notwithstanding. A brilliant engineer, businessman and musician, he would have had to forget his accomplishments and swallow his pride in order to learn.

I had to swallow both my pride and my hydrophobia when at 40 I decided to learn to swim. I couldn't believe that my instructor wanted me to get into three feet of water on my first day at the pool! I held on tightly to his hands as he got me on my stomach to teach me how to kick my feet. For the next few days I was not a pretty sight as I fought the water at the Mecklenburg County Aquatic Center in full view of some much younger and expert swimmers, swallowing an unholy amount of chlorinated water in the process.

I endured the humiliation and grew my fins.

It did not take long after I convinced my son to stay on the saddle that he was happily pedaling away. I was confident enough to let him mount the bicycle because I knew there were things he was bringing to this experience that would help him learn. Perhaps the most important was a couple of years of walking experience from which he had learnt balance and motion.

He needed neither a certificate from the Academy of Balance and Mobility nor the balancing ability of a tightrope walker to qualify to sit on the saddle. We can over-invest in preparation and end up simply delaying the fulfillment of God's purpose for our lives. Not every task requires us to have a PhD to accomplish it. Not everything that God calls us to requires professional credentials. Pressuring the Davids of today to be graduates of West Point before attempting to confront Goliath will only serve to delay Israel's victory and to prolong her agony.

In Matthew 10, Jesus called together His disciples and sent them out to preach, to heal the sick, to cleanse the lepers, to raise the dead, and to cast out devils. They had never done it before. They were not men of letters armed with credentials in theology from a four-year seminary.

Many people are too terrified to move into their callings because like Moses, they underestimate the worth of what they already have. Acts 7:22 tells us that Moses was

> "…learned in all the wisdom of the Egyptians, and was mighty in words and deeds".

According to the Living Bible version of that same Scripture, Pharaoh's daughter had taught Moses

> *"all the wisdom of the Egyptians, and he became a mighty prince and orator".*

Yet when the Lord told Moses to go and speak to Pharaoh and deliver the children of Israel from Egyptian bondage, all of a sudden the great orator could not speak! The problem was not the supposed speech impediment. Something else was haunting Moses. It was the memory of a forty-year-old mistake, a forty-year-old act of presumption that had resulted in his exile from Egypt (Exodus 2:11-15). His failure to mobilize the Hebrews to rebel forty years earlier when he had killed an Egyptian he found abusing a Hebrew, had clearly affected his self-confidence and wounded his pride.

Some of our mistakes and failures are so old that it takes an unbelievable amount of pride to think that anyone remembers them, or that it makes any difference if they do.

Unfading memories of past failures and mistakes can be a serious hindrance to learning. The reason it took me until my forties to learn to swim was because of a near-death experience in a pool when I was a little boy. After that experience, I swore I would never get into a pool again. A few years later, I slipped and fell into a pond and just managed to pull myself out after two mouthfuls of dirty water. A few months later, determined to learn, I jumped into a river and slowly started sinking in the mud before being pulled out when it was almost too late. For almost thirty years thereafter, I made sure I stayed out of any water that was higher than my ankles.

I had to forget those experiences to muster enough courage to even set my foot in the shallow end of the pool when I finally decided to learn. I had to bury the past. If little children were to dwell on the number of times they fall as they transition from crawling to walking, they would never walk.

We must draw our confidence from the fact that God has enough confidence to sit us on the saddle. We must also see the saddle as the potter's wheel where He spins His clay into the shape that He desires for His glory. God's leaders are made in motion. He sets us on the saddle to fashion us through the dynamic motion of the calls and the molding of His hands.

Moses needed to trust that God was able not only to mold him, but also to hold him up as he struggled to master the responsibilities of his call. It is not possible to learn from the saddle without trusting the hands of the instructor.

We must believe the words of the 121st Psalm:

> *"He will not suffer thy foot to be moved:*
> *He that keepeth thee will not slumber. Behold He that*
> *keepeth Israel shall neither slumber nor sleep.*
> *The Lord is thy keeper: the Lord is thy shade upon thy*
> *right hand. The sun shall not smite thee by day, nor*
> *the moon by night. The Lord shall preserve thee from*
> *all evil: He shall preserve thy soul. The Lord shall preserve*
> *thy going out and thy coming in from this time*
> *forth, and even for evermore"* (Verses 3-8).

We can only learn in motion when we trust Him to uphold us. We develop a multidimensional and deeper understanding of the relationship between balancing and movement when we learn in motion. We often discover the hard way how much and at what speed to lean into a turn without falling over, and develop the skill to make critical judgment calls on the fly.

Like many learners, my son became so fascinated by some early successes that he forgot to watch the road. He predictably hit a brick wall. Our riding lessons would be incomplete if they did not teach us the valuable lessons of riding around obstacles.   My son found out that it was more foolish to be afraid to turn the handles than to hit an obstacle.   Sometimes he would get off the bicycle and try to remove the obstacle.   When he discovered that some obstacles were either too heavy for him to move or were simply immovable, he worked harder at learning to maneuver his way around them.

The challenges we will meet will force us to apply ourselves much harder at those things that God wants us to learn. After the disciples had failed to minister deliverance to a young man who was possessed of demons in Matthew 17, they asked Jesus why they had failed. Jesus answered in the 21st verse that the kind of demon they had encountered would not go out except "by prayer and fasting". What Jesus was saying to his disciples was clear:

Place more emphasis on fasting and praying.

After our practical lessons have shone the light on those areas where we fall short, God's expectation is that we do something to make up for our shortcomings. In Luke 19 Zacchaeus recognized that he could not see Jesus because of the crowd and because he was little of stature. His response was to climb into a sycomore tree. When he did, not only did he see Jesus, but he was also seen of Him.

Zacchaeus did something that normally would be beneath him. He was, after all, a rich publican. Yet if he was to see Jesus, he had to humble himself to climb the tree.

The disciples needed to climb the sycomore tree of fasting and prayer to cast the devil out. When we work on those things God shows us we lack, not only are we going to be able to accomplish the things we desire to accomplish, but we position ourselves for Him to see us and to invite us to further fellowship with Him.

the CHALLENGE - > Trusting the
Coach

1. How does learning from the saddle help us to know how to make critical judgments on the fly?

2. How are kingdom leaders "made in motion"?

3. How does our ability to endure the humiliation of learning help us to become what God wants us to be?

Personal lessons learned from Chapter 8

1.

2.

3.

"He will not suffer thy foot to be moved."
- Psalm 121:3

N I N E

God, Leadership
& Hierarchy

*They went
their way as a flock,
they were troubled because
there was no shepherd.*

ZECHARIAH 10:2

*We are not any less
close to God in grace
because others are closer
to Him in rank.*

O n the numerous occasions in the book of Judges when the
children of Israel cried out for deliverance, God responded not
by giving them great ideas, but by raising leaders. He even raised new
leaders to deal with crises created by leadership failure.

The entire biblical record confirms that God believes in the leadership
method. In modern times when there is a particularly egregious case
of leadership failure, we have a tendency to want to throw out the
baby with the bath water. The prophets of old were adept at dividing
the issues, speaking the truth to kings even as they honored their

offices. David would not lift up his hand against Saul, honoring him as "God's anointed", even while enduring his persecution.

It is easy to let our sense of outrage with leadership failure blind us to the fact that on balance, there is a lot of good that the leaders of yesterday and today have produced. Indeed it is impossible to point to any victory in battle or a successful collective effort that has not been the result of great human leadership. The world handed Hitler, Mussolini and Hirohito decisive thrashings during World War II because of the great leadership of Winston Churchill, Dwight D. Eisenhower and Charles de Gaulle, among others.

After the war, the visionary leadership of Konrad Adenauer, the first chancellor of West Germany, gave a vanquished and despondent nation the will to rise from ruin to become the second most dynamic economy in the world in less than a decade. In the United States, the civil rights battle would not have been won without Martin Luther King Jr. even as India's independence from Britain could not have been gained in 1947 without Mahatma Gandhi.

The Scriptures demonstrate clearly that God not only believes in the leadership method, but even associates the vulnerability of His people with the absence of leadership:

> *"And they were scattered, because there is no shepherd:*
> *and they became meat to all the beasts of the field,*
> *when they were scattered."* (Ezekiel 34:5).

According to Zechariah 10:2 the children of Israel "were troubled because there was no shepherd".

In 1 Samuel 22:2, God sent to David four hundred men who were *"in distress, and everyone that was in debt, and everyone that was discontented"*. David recognized why God had sent them to him: they needed a shepherd. They needed a leader. His response was not to become their friend or their equal in distress. He became a captain over them.

While their condition was a result of the failure of leadership (Saul's) they understood that it would take submission to leadership (David's) to change their lot.

In the book of Romans, the apostle Paul's statement in defense of the leadership method could not have been stronger:

> *"Let every soul be subject unto the higher powers. For there is no power but of God: the powers that be are ordained of God. Whosoever therefore resisteth the power, resisteth the ordinance of God: and they that resist shall receive to themselves damnation. For rulers are not a terror to good works, but to the evil. Wilt thou then not be afraid of the power? do that which is good, and thou shalt have praise of the same"* (Romans 13:1-3).

In addition to the leadership method, we can trace the origins of hierarchic organization to God. Our concerns over issues of liberty and equality notwithstanding, the evidence of God's authorship of hierarchic organization is irrefutable.

God's designation of man as the lead species with dominion over the rest of His creation (Genesis 1:26-28) suggests hierarchic organization. Colossians 1:16 tells us that He created all things in heaven and in earth, including thrones, dominions, principalities and powers [kings, kingdoms, rulers, and authorities (NLT) and powers, authorities, lords and rulers (NCV)].

The sitting arrangements John saw in heaven (Revelation 4:2-4) suggested hierarchy and rank. Set in heaven was a single throne, surrounded by twenty-four seats on which sat twenty-four elders with crowns of gold on their heads. These elders clearly occupied a place of special rank and privilege.

God did not institute hierarchic organization to benefit those who sit at the top. Colossians 1:16 makes it clear that all things, including the thrones, dominions principalities and powers were created by Him *"for Him"*. God is as unhappy with self-serving and abusive leaders as those who are victimized by them. He is equally unhappy with the rebellious who *"despise dominion, and speak evil of dignities"* (Jude 8).

While the injustice of any system that produces inequality of worth must rightfully be condemned, God's non-egalitarian ordering of His troops is not meant to create second-class citizens of the kingdom. In God's kingdom, inequality of rank is not inequality of worth. While those who are lower in rank might sit at a greater distance from the throne, no one is any less close to God in grace because others are closer to Him in rank. The purpose of hierarchic organization is to produce the dynamic inequalities that compel the agenda of any social or spiritual grouping forward. He raises some above others to provoke systemic imbalances that are necessary to overcome institutional and organizational inertia.

Our opinions of hierarchic organization usually change with our position in it. When we occupy the lower ranks, it is easy to think of a hierarchical system as unjust. Our view often changes dramatically when we are at the top. It bears remembering that according to Isaiah 14:12-14, Satan was ejected from heaven because of his dissatisfaction with where he was on God's pecking order. He was cut to the ground because he had said in his heart

"I will ascend into heaven, I will exalt my throne above the stars of God: I will sit also upon the mount of the congregation, in the sides of the north; I will ascend above the heights of the clouds; I will be like the Most High" (verse 13).

Satan's focus was all wrong. His preoccupation with upward mobility led him to try to rise above those God had set above him. His ultimate goal was to *"preside on the mountain of the gods"* (The New Living Translation) in a position of equality with God.

In God's kingdom, it is God who does the promoting. Our responsibility is to hunker down in humility where He has placed us and focus our energies on moving His agenda forward. Psalm 75:5-7 is clear on that score:

"Lift not up your horn on high: speak not with a stiff neck. For promotion cometh neither from the east, nor from the west, nor from the south. But God is the judge: he putteth down one, and setteth up another."

Where God places us in His hierarchical formation, and when He chooses to promote us is His sovereign prerogative. Because he could not wait upon God for promotion, the judgment upon Satan was swift and sure: he was evicted from heaven and consigned to the dark depths of hell.

The same judgment befell those angels that followed in his rebellion:

"And the angels which kept not their first estate, but left their own habitation, he hath reserved in everlasting chains under darkness unto the judgment of the great day." (Jude 6).

Today the idea of "keeping the first estate" (being content with limited authority, our position in God's hierarchy and with what we have) is a difficult proposition for an impatient generation that prefers the gospel of instant results to the gospel of process. Driven by desire for honor, power and money, we are deceived by the enemy into despising God's efforts to lay a sure foundation for our lives and calls.

We are admonished in Zechariah 4:10 not to despise the day of small beginnings. When God positions us anywhere in His hierarchy, it does not mean He is going to leave us there forever. What He wants is to lay a foundation of humility before He lifts us up (1 Peter 5: 5-6):

> "...be clothed with humility: for God resisteth the proud, and giveth grace to the humble. Humble yourselves therefore under the mighty hand of God, that he may exalt you in due time:"

We must be without covetousness in our conduct, and be content with our station in life because according to Proverbs 3:33-34 His blessings are not dependent on rank but on righteousness:

> "He blesseth the habitation of the just. Surely He scorneth the scorners: but He giveth grace unto the lowly."

We have a tendency to demand promotion when what we must have is more faith. After Jesus "promoted" the disciples and sent them out to minister by themselves, they were stumped by a demon in Matthew 17 and were rebuked by Jesus for their faithlessness. It is not the rank that does the job, but the faith that we possess. Steven's life proved that case beyond a reasonable doubt. Chosen in Acts 6 to be a deacon whose responsibility was to take care of food distribution, he would not let his low rank relative to the apostles' stop him from doing great exploits for God:

> *"And Stephen, full of faith and power, did great wonders and miracles among the people."* (Acts 6:8)

Clearly the power that makes a kingdom difference has nothing to do with rank but with faith. We become effective in the kingdom when we accept God's order and fight the battle confident that what matters is not our rank but our faith.

the CHALLENGE - > Accepting God's order

1. What is the scriptural basis for the statement that we are not any less close to God in grace because others are closer to Him in rank?

2. How would the absence of a hierarchical structure undermine an army's effectiveness in carrying out its job?

3. If God is the author of hierarchic organization and its inherent inequalities, is it possible for the Gospel to speak to issues of social justice?

Personal lessons learned from Chapter 9

1.

2.

3.

"Let every soul be subject unto the higher powers."
- Romans 13:1

TEN

The Challenge
Of Trouble

*While leaders may be called
from their mothers' wombs,
they are molded
in the furnace of affliction.*

We must see in trouble the opportunity to begin.

If anything good can be said about trouble, it is that nothing imposes clarity of vision and compels efficiency of action quite like it. In addition, it wakes us up to the importance of leadership and heightens our sense of social responsibility.

The events of 9/11 will go down not just as a bloodstain on the pages of history, but also for its impact on leadership. The decade that preceded the tragedy had a profound impact on the practice of leadership. The roaring nineties had charged forward at a pace that defied direction, producing the kind of results on the economic front no leader could claim responsibility for without sounding ridiculous. Those who dared were roundly berated for being delusional megalomaniacs.

Al Gore will forever regret ever claiming to have been the father of the internet.

What we seemed to be witnessing was the advancing of society to a post-modern level of self-directing dynamism where leaders were largely irrelevant. To many modernists, such a society - with its promise of unfettered economic growth driven by technological innovation - was the best guarantor of the economic welfare of the people.

Educated, economically empowered and armed with their civil rights, many were becoming increasingly uncomfortable with the idea of leadership and hierarchical relationships. To accommodate the sensibilities of the times, some Christian leaders began to subscribe to a theology of leadership that denounced structure, hierarchy and leadership as enemies of a productive liberty in Christ.

The 2000 American presidential election took place in this ideological context. After winning the election, President George W. Bush went on to assemble a cabinet of strong leaders whose pain was evident as they struggled for several months to figure out how to lead in an age that was uncomfortable with being led. Sensing the administration's disorientation, it was not long before rumors began to circulate in the press of an imminent Donald Rumsfeld resignation.

Time magazine in its cover story published a day before 9/11 asked the pertinent question concerning the general who seemed to have disappeared into the mist at Foggy Bottom:

"Where Have You Gone, Colin Powell?"

If the bursting of the internet bubble had shaken the people's confidence in the economic wisdom of the new ideology, September

11 emphatically demonstrated the tragic vulnerabilities thereof. As the day's events unfolded almost in slow motion, yesterday's "egomaniacs" were transformed into the day's heroes as they boldly stepped forward to offer guidance to a grieving nation. Pastors and rabbis who had been increasingly marginalized were invited back to center stage to help the nation make sense of it all. Ordinary people heard the call to service in the rumble of the collapsing buildings and in the voice of the nation's pain. Time magazine's choice of Rudolph Giulliani as "Person of the Year" and President George Bush's popularity even among liberals could not have represented the new attitude towards leadership any better.

In an article titled *The Case for Rage and Retribution* carried in a special issue of Time magazine dedicated to September 11, Lance Morrow wrote:

> "America, in the spasms of a few hours, became a changed country. It turned the corner, at last, out of the 1990s. The menu of American priorities was rearranged. The presidency of George W. Bush begins now. What seemed important a few days ago... became instantly trivial".

As a sign of the new times (Time December 2001 issue p.120), President George W. Bush "has presided over the greatest expansion in federal power in a generation or more." Opinion polls that only a few months before had shown a majority of Americans highly distrustful of federal authority now showed a majority favoring the President's expansion of the reach of the federal government. Conservatives and liberals in Congress became almost indistinguishable as they passed bills that gave the government a broad range of policing powers in the interest of state security. Democrats who had been unhappy with the outcome of the 2000 presidential elections began calling George Bush "our President," and three weeks after the attack, Al Gore declared that George Bush was his Commander-In-Chief!

Once America allowed her leaders to lead, in short order, the Taliban government that had harbored America's enemies in Afghanistan for over a decade was gone, followed by the regime of the Iraqi strongman Saddam Hussein. For years, the terrorist networks that brought the day of trouble to America had been allowed to strengthen themselves even as America's leaders were struggling to exercise power during changing times. It took the day of trouble to turn the tide.

We must see in our trouble the opportunity and the call to begin. When we allow trouble to victimize us, we become unable to take hold of our destiny. Joseph's dream would never have been fulfilled without his day of trouble. Had he chosen to be too messed up to interpret the dreams of the jailed servants of Pharaoh, his gift would never have been brought to the attention of Egypt's ruler, and Joseph would never have risen to the exalted position which was his destiny.

For June Scobee the day of trouble arrived suddenly on the morning of the 28th of January 1986. The wife of space shuttle Challenger Commander Francis R. (Dick) Scobee watched in horror as the shuttle carrying her husband and six other crewmembers blew up two minutes into the flight of what was supposed to be a historic mission. Barely three months after the Challenger disaster, June Scobee launched the Challenger Center for Space Science Education. Her network of 40 Challenger Learning Centers reaches 500,000 students each year.

For John Walsh, host of America's number one crime-fighting show America's Most Wanted, a highly successful career as an advocate for victims' rights began with a tragic personal loss. On July 27, 1981, John and Reve Walsh's six-year-old son Adam was abducted and later

The Challenge Of Trouble 97

found murdered. The tragedy interrupted John Walsh's career as a partner in a Florida-based hotel management company and altered the course of his family's life forever.

John and Reve Walsh heard in the tragedy the call of a cause to which they have since dedicated their lives. Their advocacy was to lead, a year after Adam's murder, to the passage of the Missing Children's Act of 1982, and three years later the Missing Children's Assistance Act of 1984, which led to the establishment of the National Center for Missing and Exploited Children. The center has since its launch helped reunite over 46,000 missing children with their families, and John Walsh's crime fighting efforts through his television program have to date been credited with the capture of over 600 fugitives.

Chuck Colson became one of the great Christian leaders of our time after serving time in prison for his part in the improprieties of the Nixon administration. He would not let the devil convince him that the Lord's outstretched hand of redemption was unreachable from the depth of the pit he had dug himself.

We can rise to the challenge of leadership from bankruptcy or from Davidic, Clintonesque or Nixonian moral failure. We must see in trouble a testing ground for our faith and gifts, and discover our responsibility to others in the pain of our loss.

What the devil intends to do through trouble is to cripple us through fear. To accomplish that, he gives trouble a soundtrack and a megaphone. The prophet Zephaniah calls the day of trouble "a day of the trumpet" (Zephaniah 1:15-16). Indeed sound is trouble's outstretched hand, extending its reach beyond ground zero, and widening the field in which its consequences are felt.

The sound of this trumpet achieves in those that are fearful the same results as the actual experience of trouble.   In II Samuel 4:1, we read about the effect of the news of Abner's demise in Hebron on the son of Saul in Israel:

> *"And when Saul's son heard that Abner was dead in Hebron, his hands were feeble, and all the Israelites were troubled".*

In Joshua 2:11, Rahab tells the Hebrews of the impact of the news of their advancing towards Jericho:

> *"And as soon as we heard these things, our hearts did melt, neither did there remain any more courage in any man, because of you".*

By itself, the voice of trouble is a deadly blow to the fearful. To make sure that we are out for the count, the enemy catches us off guard with the suddenness of the blow.   Proverbs 3:25 tells us that those who have confidence in God cannot be afraid of "sudden trouble" (NVC).   The faith response cannot just be reserved for the trouble we anticipate, but must be evident even when things go wrong suddenly.

The God in whom we believe is not shaken by the suddenness with which bad things happen to us. We must remain confident that He will keep our foot from being taken even when we face the "sudden fear that troubleth" referred to in Job 22:10. The choice between succumbing to fear of "the spoiler that shall suddenly come" (Jeremiah 6:26) and having confidence in the Lord would be easy if we were always able to allow our knowledge of God's faithfulness to inform our responses.   It is imperative that we train ourselves to respond in faith to the suddenness of trouble, lest when the Lord's day shall come suddenly, we too shall be overtaken by it like the children of disobedience (1 Thessalonians 5:1-3/Luke 21:25-26).

Fear ensures that we do not respond to trouble as God wants us to. We must hear in the sound and suddenness of trouble an urgent call to duty, and respond with a clear vision of what must be done.

the CHALLENGE -

Finding purpose in trouble

1. What compromises our ability to respond to trouble the way the Lord wants us to respond?

2. When Satan would cast forth the seed of trouble into the lives of God's children in the Scriptures, how did they transform it into the seed of a divine testimony?

3. How does trouble rearrange the menu of our priorities?

Personal lessons learned from Chapter 10

1.
2.
3.

"The Lord hear thee in the day of trouble; the name of the God of Jacob defend thee."

- Psalms 20:1

Frontline Leadership

*...cursed be he that
keepeth back his
sword from blood.*

JEREMIAH 48:10

*We cannot survive frontline leadership
without the faith that enables us
to discern the invisible firewall
of God's protection.*

Every so often events will conspire to set fire to our hiding places, making it impossible for us to run away from the responsibility of frontline leadership. In the first decade of the 21st Century, the assault on Christian and family values has set the jungle of political correctness ablaze, leaving no place of retreat for those who may be tempted to go back to a benign and politically correct gospel.

We cannot afford to continue keeping the sharp edges of the Gospel hidden when the enemy has unsheathed his own weapons. As the Goliath of the liberal movement continues to challenge God's people, each generation must take the cue from the Davidic actions of the few who insist on raising the banner of Christ high.

In February 2004, the hero of the faith was an unlikely one: an erstwhile action movie star by the name of Mel Gibson. Like David, Gibson boldly stepped onto the frontlines, unsheathed the sword of truth in the form of a blockbuster movie called *The Passion of The Christ*, and dared us to do the same. Like Israel's fighting men who had scattered before Goliath to hide, we have a responsibility to leap onto the frontlines to seize the moment:

> *"And the men of Israel and of Judah arose, and shouted, and pursued the Philistines, until thou come to the valley, and to the gates of Ekron. And the wounded of the Philistines fell down by the way to Shaaraim, even unto Gath, and unto Ekron."* 1 Samuel 17:52.

We must understand that the frontlines are places for action, and not for controversy. We must resist the temptation to digress into unproductive controversies about the worthiness of the people who show us the way. The fact that David was a boy did not stop Saul's generals from jumping onto the frontlines once Goliath was slain, just as Gibson's "lack of credentials" in Christian leadership should not provide an excuse for us not to seize the moment.

Both Gibson and his movie modeled the kind of frontline leadership that makes moral neutrality impossible. We heard in the voice of the movie the prophet Elijah's challenge to a double-minded people:

> *"And Elijah came unto all the people, and said, How long halt ye between two opinions? if the LORD be God, follow him: but if Baal, then follow him."* 1 Kings 18:21.

If the most modest efforts to uphold Christian ideals triggers as much controversy as we have seen in recent years, it follows that any genuine response to the call of any kingdom cause will necessarily place us at the frontlines, face to face with an enemy whose mission to steal, kill and destroy (John 10:10) will never change until the coming of Christ.

A friend observed recently that biblical Christians are going to be facing ever more pressures as they become ever more politically incorrect. The reality is that becoming more politically incorrect will not necessarily be the result of being more radical, but will often simply be the crime of obedience and continuing to believe what we believe.

Once we are on the frontlines, we can neither keep our weapons sheathed nor withhold them from shedding blood. Jeremiah 48: 10 tells us that those who keep their swords from shedding blood are cursed. David unsheathed the sword of the Spirit to respond to Goliath's challenge, and thrust at him with the word of the Lord:

> *"...Thou comest to me with a sword, and with a spear, and with a shield: but I come to thee in the name of the LORD of hosts, the God of the armies of Israel, whom thou hast defied. This day will the LORD deliver thee into mine hand; and I will smite thee, and take thine head from thee; and I will give the carcases of the host of the Philistines this day unto the fowls of the air, and to the wild beasts of the earth; that all the earth may know that there is a God in Israel. And all this assembly shall know that the LORD saveth not with sword and spear: for the battle is the LORD's, and he will give you into our hands."* (1 Samuel 17:45-47).

The battle was won with the sword of the Spirit even before the slingshot.

When we are on the frontline we are in the line of fire. What we must be able to discern are the invisible walls of God's protection. Proverbs 18:10 tells us that the name of the Lord is a strong tower into which the righteous run and are safe. It was David's armor in his battle against the giant. Whereas the Philistine came to him "with a sword and with a spear and with a shield", he came in the protection of the invisible walls of the name of the Lord of hosts.

We often feel vulnerable because when we fight from behind the protection of an invisible wall, the enemy can see us as much as we can see him. It takes the eye of faith to discern the invisible presence of God's protection. Those who cannot see it have a difficult time feeling secure. In 2 Kings 6, Elisha's servant could not see it. Surrounded by the host the king of Syria had sent to capture his master and him, he turned to Elisha and cried in fear:

> *"...Alas, my master! how shall we do? And he answered, Fear not: for they that be with us are more than they that be with them. And Elisha prayed, and said, LORD, I pray thee, open his eyes, that he may see. And the LORD opened the eyes of the young man; and he saw: and, behold, the mountain was full of horses and chariots of fire round about Elisha."* (verses 15-17).

We cannot survive frontline leadership without the faith that enables us to discern the invisible firewall of God's protection. When we are preoccupied with dodging bullets that will never reach us, we will be unable to fulfill God's purpose for our lives.

In Numbers 13 and 14, Joshua and Caleb were prepared to lead the charge into the land of the giants because they did not doubt God's protection for His own in battle. After returning to the congregation of Israel in the wilderness of Paran from spying out the Promised Land, they were not afraid to contradict the negative report brought back by the ten men who had been in their spying party. After being swayed by the negative report, the people had spoken of choosing another leader to replace Moses to lead them back to Egypt. Outraged, Joshua and Caleb had responded:

> "...The land, which we passed through to search it, is an exceeding good land. If the LORD delight in us, then he will bring us into this land, and give it us; a land which floweth with milk and honey. Only rebel not ye against the LORD, neither fear ye the people of the land; for they are bread for us: their defense is departed from them, and the LORD is with us: fear them not." Numbers 14:7-9

The statement: *"their defense is departed from them, and the LORD is with us"* tells us that Joshua and Caleb could see what others could not. They could see the firewall around them.

When the congregation spoke of stoning them in the tenth verse, the firewall appeared:

> "But all the congregation bade stone them with stones. And the glory of the LORD appeared in the tabernacle of the congregation before all the children of Israel."

Frontline leaders can count on the protection of the firewall even from the stone throwing of their own. We must be as unafraid of those we lead as we are of engaging the enemy in battle. Joshua and Caleb were frontliners both at home and on the battlefield. They were as passionate about truth to their own as they were about advancing God's purpose on the battlefield. To be confident and effective on any battlefield, they had to trust God's hedge of protection.

Frontline leaders respond to the call of the cause even when those who will benefit do not appreciate it. Several years ago, the discovery that we had six to twelve-year-olds in our children's church who could not read or write was heartbreaking. The need was very clear and very real to us. We had established the children's church for inner city children to lay a moral foundation upon which they could build a life of responsibility, but clearly our intervention needed to be comprehensive enough to also address their educational needs.

We came up with a plan we were sure would receive the enthusiastic support of the parents, grandparents and guardians of the children: We would establish a private Christian school for underprivileged children with generous financial aid for all students.

During the effort to sign up some students for the school, an elderly lady responded before slamming the door in our faces:

"I don't want my grandchild attending no private school."

When the grandparent of another troubled child said the same thing, I asked her if she did not agree that her grandchild was not doing well in the school where he was. She agreed. Was she concerned about his behavior? She said she was. Did she not think he would benefit from a smaller class size, qualified teachers, great curriculum, and a morally based education etc? She thought he would. Would she sign up for the school then?

No.

As we were leaving, she shouted behind us: "Hey…do y'all have meat at your food bank?"

The world's demand that we respond to its need on its terms is nothing new. Neither is its insistence that we respond to the needs it perceives, rather than what God shows us it needs. When I was sick as a child, my father's solution was hardly what I thought I needed. He would walk me to the small country clinic where he and the large nurse would proceed to wrestle me to the table. I would put up quite a fight as the nurse with her elbow and her weight on my back would measure the medicine in the injection. Worried that the needle might break from my thrashing around, my father would resort to the only thing he knew worked to calm me down - repeated slaps to my bare bottom as the nurse picked just the right moment to plunge the huge needle in during my final scream of protest. She would soothe me afterwards with the candy that she kept in the clinic for just these kinds of situations.

I did not think it was an act of love for my father to take me to that clinic. Yet it was more than that. I owe that nurse my life, as I do my parents. I have no doubt that my father hated taking me to the clinic because he knew I hated it. Yet it was all part of the responsibility of leadership he could not run away from.

The one thing the enemy does successfully is to make the world hate the treatment more than the sickness, the Savior more than the deceiver. It is part of the deception through which he accomplishes his destructive mission. He encourages the world to write its own prescriptions, to be its own healer. The challenge of frontline leadership is to provide God's prescription to a world that needs it, yet violently rejects it.

God gave His Son because He knew that the world needed a savior, not because they either wanted or demanded Him. When we, like God, choose to give the world what it needs but what it does not necessarily want, we can set off a storm of controversy. Had God chosen to avoid the controversy by not giving us a savior, we would all be living under condemnation today. To be sure, the controversy still rages, as do the triumphs, the decisions for the Lord, the deliverances and the accomplishing of His redemptive purposes.

It frustrates the enemy that frontliners win even when they "lose". It confounds the wisdom of the wise that Jesus "lost" the battle and changed the world. In the natural, they stopped Him. In the natural they prevailed at the cross. Little did they know that they had to win the battle in order for Him to win the greater victory: that His ultimate triumph had to be victory over their own "victory".

It scares the enemy to know that no matter what level of success he may achieve, he will always lose. It scares him that frontliners shall arise in our time who will say that fighting the homosexual agenda is a battle they would feel honored to fight and "lose", the Stephen (Acts 7:54-60) and John (Mark 6:15-29) kind of leaders who understand that there is victory even in what may seem like an inglorious death.

We have a duty to respond to the call for frontline leadership. As we have seen in recent times, when we fail to respond, the frontlines will come into our homes, our schools, our churches and our jobs. Since we still pay a price for not acting, we might just as well draw our swords.

the CHALLENGE - > Draw your sword!

1. Is there any inconsistency between preaching grace and presenting double-edged truth?

2. Can a genuine response to the call of the cause place us anywhere else but on the frontlines?

3. Why is being more politically incorrect not necessarily the result of being more radical?

Personal lessons learned from Chapter 11

1.
2.
3.

"But the youth drew not his sword; for he feared, because he was yet a youth."

- Psalms 20:1

TWELVE

The World
In Which We Live

*Frontliners cannot operate on
assumptions about the world
in which they live,
they must operate on truth.*

*Civil society is civil to everything
but the truth of the Gospel*

O ur responses to the causes of our times must be appropriate to
the world and the times in which we live. To provide definition
to our leadership, we must know the nature of our world and where
we are on God's calendar.

Is this a time for celebrating the unlimited possibilities promised
by the scientific and technological advances of our time, or are we
living in a dark time where *"all the foundations of the earth are out of
course"* (Psalm 82:5), a time of imminent judgment as Babylon's cup
of disobedience fills to overflowing?

We are unlikely to see the true nature of the world if we are blinded
by our love for it. The last thing a world in crisis needs are the self-

canceling efforts of a schizophrenic leadership corps that cannot make up its mind whether it's of the world or not. The Scripture tells us in 1 John 2:15-16:

> *"Love not the world, neither the things that are in the world. If any man love the world, the love of the Father is not in him."*

It is our love for God that will enable us to see the darkness of our world and of our socio-economic and political systems. Human progress has not made us more able to rid the world of sin, but simply to disguise the stench. We dress a fallen culture with the civilized covering of modernity so we can mine its "riches" without the distraction of a nagging conscience. We forget that the God in whom there is no *"deceivableness of unrighteousness"* (2 Thessalonians 2:10) cannot be fooled by either the packaging or by our insistence that we have somehow managed to build a better world out of bricks baked in the kiln of liberal humanism.

We cannot offer God an alternative version of goodness that is at variance with His own. He needs no help from us understanding what is good and what is not. He will neither be compelled nor duped to see goodness in a world in which He does not see Himself.

Jesus instructed His disciples not to love their world because He did not see much good in it. What He saw was a dark place in need of light. He and His band of disciples were the light their world rejected and was determined to snuff out (John 1:6-11/Matthew 5:14). The disciples were the light not because they were great scientists or great humanitarians, but because of the truth of the word that had been committed to them:

> *"I have given them thy word; and the world hath hated them, because they are not of the world, even as I am not of the world.*

I pray not that thou shouldest take them out of the world, but that thou shouldest keep them from the evil. They are not of the world, even as I am not of the world. Sanctify them through thy truth: thy word is truth. As thou hast sent me into the world, even so have I also sent them into the world." (John 17:14-18).

A world that rejected truth then was a world in darkness.   Similarly a world that rejects truth today is a world in darkness, its technological and socio-economic advances notwithstanding. As societies advance, their desire for the light of God's word diminishes significantly. As a result, the Gospel has increasingly become unwelcome not just in the "closed" societies of the Moslem world, but even in the "civilized" and "free" liberal democracies of western Europe and yes…increasingly even in the United States. We are sometimes discovering too late that civil society is civil to everything else except the truth of the Gospel.

As we become part of a larger global reality, we have every reason to be concerned that it is primarily a liberal agenda that drives the international effort to build "civil societies". We become the unwitting agents of liberal internationalism when we drink indiscriminately from the trough of any international movement that claims to be a champion of civil rights and democracy.

The international liberal movement is a force to reckon with, as any nation that has sought to defend its right to define its moral values has discovered. It is a movement that has arrogated to itself the right to impose its values on everybody, and through the international financial and aid organizations that it controls, generously rewards those countries that are most receptive to its ideals, while harshly punishing those who are not.

It is out of the international liberal constituency, which has been built over the years through the aggressive efforts of an ultra-liberal

Europe, that leaders of international organizations such as the United Nations, World Health Organization, World Bank, International Monetary Fund etc. are drawn.

Our inability to speak out against liberal internationalism only strengthens a system whose ultimate objective is to crown the god of humanism and establish a kingdom that will ultimately be impenetrable to the Gospel. Slaying the giant of liberal internationalism is a cause to which we must respond. To do so, we will first have to stop pretending on their behalf that the democratic societies of Western Europe are Christian nations.

Frank Bruni of the New York Times quoted in an article that appeared in Agape Press titled "The Withering of Christianity in Europe" suggests that all that is left of Christianity in Europe is "…a series of tourist-trod monuments to Christianity's past," noting that only one in 20 people bother to go to church anymore in France. Some figures put the numbers in the United Kingdom at less than 1 in 60 (compared to the United States ratio of 1 in 3.) When US Supreme Court Justice Anthony Kennedy suggested after the court had struck down a Texas law against sodomy, that "it might be time for the United States to start adopting a more European view of what constitutes right and wrong," what he was saying was that America must refuse to be bound by the truth and morality of God's word. What he was advocating was a rejection of Proverbs 22:28 (*"Remove not the ancient landmark, which thy fathers have set"*) and a complete repudiation of the Judeo-Christian foundation upon which American nation was established.

Bishop Hilarion of Vienna and Austria in an address to the 12th Assembly of the Conference of European Orthodox Churches (June 30th, 2003, Trondheim, Norway) says concerning Christianity in Europe:

"In European secular society Christian values are being more and more marginalized, God is being driven to the outskirts of human existence (the fact that God did not find place in the recently adopted European Constitutional Treaty is indicative of this tendency). It is now almost taken for granted that religion can exist only at a private level: you are free to believe in God or not, but this should in no way be manifested in your social life. Churches and religious communities are tolerated as long as they do not trespass their own borders and do not publicly express opinions that differ from those consonant with 'political correctness': should they begin to express such opinions, they are readily accused of intolerance."

After the fall of the Berlin Wall, most of the nations of the former Eastern bloc actively sought to be integrated into the European community of nations. While that may have boded well for the advancement of democracy, we must justifiably be concerned about the expansion of a Western European culture that is anti-God.

Frontline Christian leaders cannot operate on assumptions about the world in which they live. They must operate on truth. The truth is that Western Europe today, with its high standard of living, needs the Gospel more than many third world countries. Instead of focusing only on trying to "free people" from the "slavery and bondage" and "legalism" of third world Christianity (and sometimes doing much harm to the last bastions of traditional family values and simple faith in the process), missionaries will have to redirect some of their efforts to a continent that has the wherewithal to do much harm to the cause of Christ. Indeed, the small pockets of Christian activity in Western European countries, mainly in minority communities from the Third World, will need the strong support of the world Christian movement as they hold up the torch of the Gospel in hostile territory.

Can America count on the vast expanse of the Atlantic or her military might to keep her from going the way of Europe? Hardly. The corrosive rot of liberalism is as much within as it is without, slowly but surely eating away at the very core of the Christian belief system. We cannot afford to pin all our hopes on modern worship and marketing to rescue the faith and to withstand this unrelenting assault. While churches may be filled as a result of great marketing strategies, it will take all the spiritual resources of the Christian movement and a strong commitment to truth to win the war.

To understand the world in which we live, one must have an understanding of where it is coming from. It will be difficult for the millennium generation to hear the call of the cause to fight against national and international liberalism without the illuminating sense of history that gives meaning to a cause. The challenge is how to rally troops from a largely a-historical generation that finds little inspiration from the larger issues of history, and is the product of a time whose frenetic pace is hardly an ideal incubator of historical purpose.

This is a generation that pays just enough attention to the events of the times to extract what the business of the day demands. Because it is a generation that did not conspire in the great social iniquities of yesterday on which the word 'evil' hangs (slavery, segregation, etc.) and from which some of the inequities of today derive, they are driven neither by guilt nor a sense of righteous indignation to put things right.

It is hard to see it as a generation of revolutionaries, not because it does not have the capacity to dramatically affect the way things are, but because it is more comfortable with utilizing its skills to ensure that the kingdom gets its "fair share" of what postmodernism has to offer. The difficulty is not with getting it to offer its technological skills to the local church. The difficulty is getting it to train its weapons on a force that has not only scored innumerable cultural victories, but manages to consolidate its position by transforming these victories into legal, economic and political power at home and in the world at large.

It is a generation that must become convinced that it does matter who occupies the White House and who drives the agenda of international politics. In Acts 25, the apostle Paul, recognizing that being turned over to the Jews in Jerusalem to face some trumped up charges would result in certain death, was forced to choose between certain death and an only slightly better chance of obtaining justice from Caesar. Can this generation rise up to the challenge of political leadership so that when Paul appeals to Caesar, he might find in the highest courts of power people who share his beliefs?

As the story goes, all Paul's appeal to Caesar was able to buy him was a bit more time before an inevitable appointment with the gallows. The author of the book of Proverbs would tell you that it does matter who hears your cause:

> *"When the righteous are in authority, the people rejoice: but when the wicked beareth rule, the people mourn."* (Proverbs 29:2).

Somehow out of this generation must emerge great national and international jurists, political leaders and civil servants who have a clear historical perspective and are committed to fighting for Judeo-Christian values. We cannot afford to be so afraid of being swallowed up by the dragon the political process has become to concede the playing field to those who are committed to the complete dismantling of everything that is based on Christian values.

The psalmist's question deserves an answer:

> *"When foundations are being destroyed, what can the upright do?"* (Psalm 11:3 NABWRNT)

We cannot merely shrug our shoulders in response and play with our electronic devices. Confident in the faith in which we stand, we must jump into the trenches of socio-political and economic activity, knowing that truth will triumph as we fight to take back lost ground in the battle to define the world in which we live.

the CHALLENGE - > Know your world!

1. Where are we on God's calendar?

2. What are some of the practical challenges of being a leader in a world that is at war with the kingdom of God?

3. How did Daniel and his friends avoid having their faith compromised by their positions in the government of Babylon?

Personal lessons learned from Chapter 12

1.

2.

3.

"I pray not that thou shouldest take them out of the world, but that thou shouldest keep them from the evil."

- John 17:15

THIRTEEN

Discerning the Kingpins

*God is calling
us to the kind of leadership
that can discern the real power
behind the way things are.*

*We cannot discern the
kingpins without balancing
zeal with knowledge*

The British Luxury liner had been declared unsinkable. On its maiden voyage from Liverpool, England to New York, it struck an iceberg about 95 miles south of Newfoundland and sank within three hours. 1,513 of the more than 2,220 people on board lost their lives, and the Titanic disaster went down in history as one of the worst maritime disasters ever.

When the Titanic set sail, it was obviously the captain's intention to take his passengers to their destination. When we set off on the journey of leadership, our goal is to get where God wants us to get. Yet our intentions cannot guarantee that we will get where we want to go. There are real impediments on the way. Paul writes in 1

Corinthians 16:9:

> *"…a great door and effectual is opened unto me, and
> there are many adversaries".*

Note that Paul says there were adversaries (plural). The fact that there were "many adversaries" to one open door underscored the enemy's determination to stop Paul from accomplishing his goals.

To go past the enemy, God's people will have to fight with the best weapons they can find. We will have to arm ourselves with a more substantive faith than the fools' gold that is a distinguishing feature of much of contemporary Christianity.

The promises of God are not easily possessed because it is the enemy's self-appointed job to interdict us. It took several years beyond Saul's death for David to consolidate his rule over Israel because the enemy would not let him.

Since Saul had died, the obvious question would be: which enemy?

The Scriptures make it clear that the fall of Saul did not mean the end of "the house of Saul." The kingpin that held everything together was not Saul. We read in 2 Samuel 2:5-10 that when David tried to extend his rule beyond Hebron to include Jabesh-gilead, Abner who was a general in the late king's army, took Ishbosheth the son of Saul to Mahanaim and made him king over Gilead and all of Israel. That triggered a *"long war between the house of Saul and the house of David"* (2 Samuel 3:1). For seven and a half years after Saul's death, Abner kept David from Zion.

Often what we perceive to be the head is nothing more than the shadow of the true head. The reason why David was only able to take the stronghold after Abner's death (2 Samuel 5:7) was because Abner was the kingpin. The reason why "the house of Saul" only crumbled after Abner's demise was because the general was the linchpin that held the system together.

We cannot count the battle to be won until the kingpin has fallen. God is calling us to the kind of leadership that can discern the real power behind the way things are so we can fight appropriately.

Disguising figureheads as kingpins is a favorite *ruse de guerre* of the evil one. By making the figureheads prominent and the kingpins invisible, he fools us into expending all our ammunition and energy on the wrong target. He watches with satisfaction as we celebrate our victories over the figureheads, knowing that as long as we are not able to discern the kingpins, we can never possess what the Lord would like us to have.

Things changed dramatically in Israel once Abner died. The news of Abner's death shook the very foundations of the house of Saul:

> "When Saul's son heard that Abner was dead in Hebron,
> his hands were feeble, and all the Israelites were troubled."
> (2 Samuel 4:1).

After Abner died, the house of Saul imploded. Ishbosheth was killed by his own generals (2 Samuel 4:5-7), and all the tribes came and gave David the kingdom. David could possess his Jerusalem and establish his kingdom because Abner was out of the way. Much blessings were released to him:

> "And David went on, and grew great, and the Lord God
> of hosts was with him. And Hiram king of Tyre sent messengers
> to David, and cedar trees, and carpenters, and masons: and they

> *built David an house. And David perceived that the Lord*
> *had established him king over Israel, and that he had exalted*
> *his kingdom for his people Israel's sake".*
> (2 Samuel 5:10-12).

Without discerning Abner and destroying him, we are not able to advance the kingdom. When we attack the figureheads, we merely provoke endless wars that drain our energy. When we strike the kingpin, we possess our Jerusalems and end the wars.

We must go beyond the formulaic approach to kingdom advancement that ignores the fact that one person's Abner will be very different from another's. We must ask the Lord in prayer, fasting and meditation to show us our own Abners so we can possess our promises.

It takes more than a zeal for war to fight the right battle. Discernment requires knowledge more than passion. This was a lesson one of my old friends had to learn the hard way.

Vernon (name changed) was a radical Christian. During his many visits to our home, his zeal for the Lord made all of us feel like unbelievers. During one church camp meeting we both attended, Vernon was excited when many people came forward to the altar for prayer at the conclusion of one of the services. He was even more thrilled when many of those who needed deliverance were set free. Nothing gave him greater joy than watching God's word in action.

When the leaders who were praying for the people at the altar seemed to be having a problem with a stubborn demon, Vernon shouted from the back of the auditorium:

"Bind the strongman!"

When the service came to a close with the possessed girl still bound, Vernon was very disappointed. He could be heard muttering in frustration that they should have bound the strongman. When the leadership asked him to come and help, Vernon jumped up and walked purposefully towards the altar, and with the help of some of his friends, took the girl to a backroom where they proceeded to "bind the strongman".

About two hours later, the young warriors trekked out of the backroom, discouraged and defeated. They had screamed at the strongman. They had told him that he was bound. They had prayed and quoted Scripture to no avail.

Vernon and his friends were subdued for the rest of the meeting.

Over the years, Vernon has come to understand that we do not win the battle by wielding slogans that are not based on a substantive knowledge of how to do warfare. He has learnt that zeal only makes a positive difference after we have, by knowledge, correctly discerned what we are dealing with.

We can learn much about how to win the battle against the prince of darkness from the word of God and from the testimonies of others. Often, the testimonies of the successes of God's people can hide the details of the hard work, the fastings, the blood sweat and tears that led up to victory. The young warriors of the faith tend to forget that God never promised that victory would come easy. They forget that wars are won through patient, informed determination, and that zeal without knowledge breeds a monochromatic spirituality that can discern neither the nuances of God's will nor the complexities of the battle.

We can only change our world if we understand the complexities of the battle, and how God desires that we fight. We fail to move forward when we make the wrong assumptions about where the power that is resisting the advance of the kingdom lies. We set ourselves up for ultimate defeat when our knowledge lags behind our zeal.

Victory is not necessarily guaranteed by the fact that our cause is right and just, but by due diligence in preparation for war. We discussed in an earlier chapter how lack of preparation should never be used as an excuse not to obey when the Lord calls us. Clearly, what God requires of us is obedience even more than preparation. That, however, does not mean that preparation is not important to God.

When the disciples failed to cast the devil out of the young demoniac in Matthew 17, Jesus told them that they had failed because that kind of demon could only be cast out through fasting and prayer. Jesus attributed their failure to their level of preparedness. They went into that battle believing that they could win simply because their cause was right and just. They failed because they had not done due diligence. They were not prepared to fight the kind of battle required by that particular situation.

On the 27th of June 1976, a group of Palestinian terrorists hijacked a French Airbus carrying almost 80 Israeli nationals and 169 non-Israelis, and commandeered it to Entebbe, Uganda. When the non-Israeli hostages were released, the Israeli Secret Service was able to debrief a majority of them after they landed at Orly International Airport in France. From the information gathered from the former hostages, they were able to determine the number of terrorists involved, how the remaining Israeli nationals were being held, and the layout of the terminal building at Entebbe Airport in Uganda where the hostages were being held. Within a few days, the commandos of the Israeli Defense Forces (IDF) had rehearsed a rescue operation in a full-scale model of Entebbe Airport. On the 3rd of July, a week after the hijacking, they flew 2,500 miles to Uganda to execute a daring and brilliant rescue mission that brought home the hostages.

Our hatred of the enemy alone is never sufficient for us to prevail. It was not zeal that made Operation Thunderbolt, which has been called the best hostage rescue operation of modern times, a success. What won the battle was preparation.

It is easy to let our zeal go ahead of our preparation. Our preparation must be battle specific, equipping us with relevant information and details for the challenge at hand. It must be informed by specific insight that enables us to discern the underpinnings of a particular challenge and the root of a problem.

When we are prepared, when through knowledge we discern the kingpins, and when we fight against them with zeal, only one outcome is guaranteed:

We win.

the CHALLENGE - > ## Sharpening your discernment

1. What are you doing to make sure you can possess your Jerusalem?

2. What made Abner such a formidable adversary?

3. What would constitute "due diligence" in Christian leadership?

Personal lessons learned from Chapter 13

1.	
2.	
3.	

> *"When Saul's son heard that Abner was dead in Hebron, his hands were feeble."*
> *- 2 Samuel 4:1*

FOURTEEN

Vision

Our investment in the development of vision
must take into account the fact that
not every cause requires
a complicated response.

In the kingdom,
there is a higher standard
for judging a vision than its ability to
attract financial resources and
the participation of others.

The room was abuzz. What a vision! At long last, someone had come up with an outreach plan everyone could really be excited about. Churches would be overflowing as thousands came to Christ. This was how evangelism was supposed to be done in modern times.

The two-week effort would involve a media blitz of television commercials, radio advertisements and billboards featuring Christian celebrities issuing an invitation to anyone who wanted to experience the power to change. They could call in to a phone bank manned by volunteers from local churches who would answer any questions and lead the callers to Christ. The names and contact information of the callers would be recorded for follow-up by churches located in the neighborhood closest to where the person lived. Several churches donated several thousands of dollars to meet the budget of the outreach. It was indeed an impressive, well thought out plan.

Present among the thirty or so Christian leaders to whom this great vision was being pitched was a group of five young people who had been involved in door-to-door evangelism in area inner-city communities. Only two months before in a two-week period, the group's one-on-one campaign had resulted in 77 adults giving their lives to the Lord. Further outreach in the same area by the same group had resulted in the establishment of a 126 member children's church. The group operated without a budget, sharing a single six-sitter vehicle to transport the ministry team and to pick up the children for the children's church.

Their presentation to the same group of Christian leaders a few weeks earlier had not generated any noticeable excitement. In fact, their request for assistance with the purchasing of a vehicle to help with the transportation of what was to them an overwhelming harvest given their limited resources, had resulted in only one suggestion from one of the leaders in attendance: he believed the group would benefit greatly from further training in evangelism. He recommended a training program his church had been through a few months before to try and get his congregation interested in evangelism. When asked what the impact of the program had been on his own church, the leader admitted that he had yet to see any results!

Excited about this new presentation, the same leader approached the group of young people and said:

"This is really a great vision, don't you think? I hope you will be able to participate because I think you can really learn something from this."

The group was among the first to volunteer to help out at the outreach. They shared in the disappointment when the phones hardly rang the first few nights of the campaign, and joined the others in the prayer room several times a day to intercede for the outreach. When the phones were largely silent for the first week of the campaign, the organizers had to change strategies. They gave each volunteer a few pages from the local phone book to call and share Christ with whoever answered. By the end of the campaign, some decisions for Christ had been made, but hardly the flood of new converts those who had been most enthusiastic about the vision had anticipated.

It is not my intention here to suggest that the campaign sighted above was a failure, but to merely use the example as a springboard for a discussion on vision. We obviously have to be careful not to judge an event solely by the expectations of others. It would certainly be wrong to suggest that God's will can only be carried out through pedestrian one-on-one efforts. However, the danger is very real that presented with the imaginative, we can patronize the ordinary and dismiss the simple effort that is God ordained.

Having said that, lets start off by looking at the word vision. What is vision? In this context and in its modern usage, it denotes the imaginative contemplation or visualization of a response to a cause. Over the years, the ability to envision has become an important requirement for leadership. The assumption is that it enables leaders to provide organized, efficient and effective responses to the call of the causes of our times.

What we must guard against, as we become more and more proficient at project planning and visioneering, is becoming less and less dependent on God. Our investment in the development of vision must take into account that not every cause requires a complicated response, and that God requires our obedience more than our ability to organize. There clearly is a higher standard for judging a vision in the kingdom than its ability to attract financial resources and the participation of others.

That standard is obedience.

It is an open secret that great organizations, ministries, and businesses have been built upon compellingly simple foundations of obedience. The biblical testimony reveals that our obedience is more important to God than the creativity with which we respond. What a study of Hebrews 11 reveals more than proficiency in visioneering is that the great men and women of faith in God's word were bond-slaves to His will.

The intention here is not to be anti-vision, but to call the visioneers to a higher ideal. Jesus articulates this higher ideal in John 5:19:

> "...Verily, verily, I say unto you, The Son can do nothing of himself, but what he seeth the Father do: for what things soever he doeth, these also doeth the Son likewise."

To fulfill the purpose of the Father for His life, Jesus did not stray from the script written in heaven, writing the testimony of His obedience in blood. For over 2000 years the fulfillment of a heavenly vision through the obedience of the Son has been the foundation of God's church and of our faith. Timeless in its impact and immeasurable in the breath, height and depth of its reach, the testimony of the Christ is defined neither by its resourcefulness nor brilliance of execution, but by the absolute determination of the Son to hit the mark.

We must move away from a humanistic self-sufficiency to a hopeless dependence on God, recognizing that it is more important to seek the Lord about how we ought to respond to the call of the cause, than to simply offer the "sacrifice" of our brilliant minds. We must allow heaven to be the inspiration for our visions. Only then can the things that we do remain faithful to God's purpose.

The Bible sends a clear warning against building without God in Psalm 127:1:

> *"Except the LORD build the house, they labour in vain that build it: except the LORD keep the city, the watchman waketh but in vain."*

The only way to ensure that those things that we build remain faithful to His purpose is to have God directly involved in the entire process. Can the brilliant minds of our time also be prayerful ones, open to receive directly from God, and to serve as delivery vehicles for a heavenly purpose?

Some will ask, how practical is that? I would ask in response: how practical was Moses' leadership? What about Joshua's and Gideon's? Deborah's, David's and Solomon's? Did they not lead liberation movements, fight wars and undertake tremendous construction projects according to a heavenly vision? We cannot use our own failure to connect to heaven to discount the fact that our visions should not only be inspired by Him, but should be a practical expression of His will.

Why is this important? We often underestimate how difficult it is going to become in our lifetime to create our way around the political, social, economic and legal obstacles that will be put in our way. We are living in times when the outlawing of much of what remains of Christian practice that is still allowable under current law is a very distinct possibility. We have pretty much lost the cultural war, and if the issuing of 4,161 marriage licenses to same-sex couples by the city of San Francisco in a space of one month (February 12 and March 12, 2004) is any indication of how fast we are losing ground, then this is hardly the time for the soft-punching projects that dazzle the enemy but hardly dent his zeal. While we may prove with our projects that Christians can live large and have a good time, we will certainly not win this war with theme park Christianity.

It will not take much creativity to come up with a design for the end time church. It will be a lean, mean fighting machine with a knock out punch, a church that will pull people out of the fire and plunder the kingdom of darkness through militant prayer. In a world where significance is measured in complexity, and the simplicity of the mission of the church has often become lost in the complexity of vision, it will take much obedience and much courage to be simple.

Proverbs 29:18 and Habakkuk 2:2 are probably the most widely quoted Scriptures in any discussion of vision. It is important to look at these Scriptures closely to see what they really refer to.

Proverbs 29:18 says:

> *"Where there is no vision, the people perish: but he that keepeth the law, happy is he."*

Usually the first part of this Scripture is quoted in isolation. When we read the verse as a whole, it is clear that the word *vision* here is referring to the prophetic revelation that results in the knowledge of God's will. It has nothing to do with project planning. The translation of the same Scripture in the New American Bible says:

> *"Without prophecy the people become demoralized;*
> *but happy is he who keeps the law."*

The New Century Version puts it this way:

> *"Where there is no word from God, people are uncontrolled, but*
> *those who obey what they have been taught are happy."*

and lastly the New Living Translation:

> *"When people do not accept divine guidance, they run wild.*
> *But whoever obeys the law is happy."*

Clearly this Scripture is not talking about the creativity of our response to the call of the cause.

Now lets look at Habakkuk 2:2:

> *"And the LORD answered me, and said, Write the vision, and*
> *make it plain upon tables, that he may run that readeth it."*

To understand the reference to vision in this Scripture, we would have to read chapter one. In the last six verses of the first chapter, the prophet Habakkuk complains to God about the prospect of the wicked Chaldeans wiping Israel out when the Chaldeans were themselves more wicked than God's chosen people. In the first verse of chapter two, he announces that he will wait for an answer from God, whereupon the Lord tells him to write down the vision He was going to show him.

The vision the prophet Habakkuk was told to write down and

to make plain was not a business project proposal. It was not the imaginative contemplation of a ministry plan, but a revelation of what God was going to do to Israel.

What is disturbing is how we claim these Scriptures for our plans, when in fact what they really refer to were His own. While the Spirit of the Lord may use such Scriptures to confirm our need to plan, it is nonetheless incumbent upon us to rightly divide them.

It is obedience that ensures that our visions do not take on a life of their own, and end up reflecting our ego rather than addressing the kingdom need. A forty million dollar building may have more to do with the ego of those who build it than a desire to win the lost. We get into mountains of vision-related debt and overwhelming financial obligations often so we can have the best building in town. When the outreach budget of a church whose mission is to win the lost is 10%, and the overhead is 90%, there is something very wrong.

God is not necessarily impressed with the expense to which we go supposedly to respond to the call of the cause. While it is obviously commendable to desire to give God our best, what God expects from us is often very different from what we offer Him.

King Saul learnt that lesson the hard way. In 1 Samuel 15:3, the prophet Samuel had brought him a message from the Lord that he was to go against the Amalekites because they had refused to allow Israel to cross their territory during their journey to the Promised Land. The instruction to King Saul could not have been clearer:

> *"Now go and smite Amalek, and utterly destroy all that they have, and spare them not; but slay both man and woman, infant and suckling, ox and sheep, camel and ass".*

Instead of doing that, we read in verses 8 and 9 that Saul

> "...*utterly destroyed all the people with the edge of the sword,
> but Saul and the people spared Agag, and the best of the sheep,
> and of the oxen, and of the fatlings, and the lambs, and all that
> was good, and would not utterly destroy them; but everything
> that was vile and refuse, that they destroyed utterly*".

Upon returning from the battle, he announced to the prophet Samuel
that he had fulfilled the commandment of the Lord. Confronted
by Samuel to explain why he had not destroyed everything, Saul's
answer was that he had spared the best for God:

> "...*the people spared the best of the sheep and of the oxen, to
> sacrifice unto the Lord thy God; and the rest we have utterly
> destroyed*" (verse 15).

Samuel's response reveals what God thinks about our best when it
does not reflect total obedience:

> "*And Samuel said, Hath the Lord as great delight in burnt
> offerings and sacrifices, as in obeying the voice of the LORD?
> Behold, to obey is better than sacrifice, and to hearken than the
> fat of rams.*" (verse 22).

The prophet Samuel characterizes Saul's effort to offer God the best
as rebellion that qualifies for severe sanctions:

> "*For rebellion is as the sin of witchcraft, and stubbornness is as
> iniquity and idolatry. Because thou hast rejected the word of the
> Lord, he hath also rejected thee from being king.*" (verse 23).

Our good intentions do not obedience make. Indeed our good

intentions may be judged by the Lord to be acts of rebellion punishable with the withdrawal of His grace from our lives. Our desire to give God our best must never supercede His requirement for obedience. We give God our best when we obey Him. That understanding must guide the process of envisioning.

What was it that was taken away from Saul when he disobeyed? We read in 1 Samuel 13:14:

> *"But now thy kingdom shall not continue",*

and in 1 Samuel 15:28:

> *"And Samuel said unto him, The LORD hath rent the kingdom of Israel from thee this day, and hath given it to a neighbor of thine, that is better than thou".*

The kingdom was taken away from Saul even though he continued on the throne for several more years after that. It is possible to sit on the thrones of our kingdoms even after the river of God's grace has stopped flowing through them. When we sever the connection between our visions and the river of God's purpose through disobedience, we end up presiding over lifeless forms of His will for our lives.

the CHALLENGE - Seeing through His eyes

1. What is the place of creativity and initiative in Christian leadership?

2. How can you apply the higher ideals contained in John 5:19 and Psalm 127:1 to the development of your own vision?

3. Is your vision hitting the mark God wants it to hit?

Personal lessons learned from Chapter 14

1.
2.
3.

"Not every cause requires a complicated response"
- Author

FIFTEEN

Leadership By Faith
And The Power Anointing

*By faith Abraham, when he was called
to go out into a place which he should
after receive for an inheritance,
obeyed; and went out, not
knowing whither he went.*

HEBREWS 11:8

*God expects us to walk
confidently in the progressive
revelation of His will.*

God loves it when we, like Abraham the father of our faith, place ourselves completely in His hands, and allow Him to guide us on our life journeys.   He takes pleasure in our faith in Him and in the demonstration of our confidence in His plans for our lives.

Genesis 12:1 tells us:

> *"Now the Lord had said unto Abram, Get thee out of thy country, and from thy kindred, and from thy father's house, unto a land that I will show thee".*

Abraham was called to uproot himself, to leave the familiar, and to separate himself from those he loved without the benefit of a Deed of Title to the Promised Land. He did not have a written contract with God in hand. He was being asked to rise up and simply obey God by faith.

Abraham was more than just the individual who bore that name. He was the head of *Abraham Incorporated.* We get a hint of the size of his entourage in Genesis 14:14. The Scripture tells us that he had three hundred and eighteen servants *"born in his own house"*, in addition to his wife and relatives. Clearly, he was not just being asked to walk by faith, but also to lead by faith.

While what God was calling Abraham to lead his family, servants and possessions out of was clear, what was not clear was the whereto of the call. According to Hebrews 11:8

> *"By faith Abraham, when he was called to go out into*
> *a place which he should after receive for an inheritance, obeyed;*
> *and he went out, not knowing whither he went."*

How does anyone, let alone a 75-year-old man, uproot a family from a stable, prosperous existence in familiar territory and inspire them to join in an uncertain journey towards an unknown destination? The Bible does not tell us how he convinced his family to follow, but they did.

God challenged Abraham to walk and lead by faith. Abraham rose to the challenge and proceeded to walk confidently in the progressive revelation of God's will. He understood that he did not have to see the destination before responding to God's call. He understood that the promise by God that the destination would be revealed as he went was as good as a clear vision of the goal. He understood that the Lord values obedience more than our ability to see the goal, *"for we walk by faith, not by sight"* (II Corinthians 5:7).

Abraham's journey oftentimes seemed to be leading him nowhere. He hit a few brick walls on the way. The Canaan he encountered after leaving Haran seemed like a dead end. No sooner had he arrived than there was a great famine. According to Genesis 12:10:

> *"...Abram went down into Egypt to sojourn there;*
> *for the famine was grievous in the land".*

This was no ordinary famine; the Scripture describes it as a grievous one. So grievous was it that he had to move on to Egypt to survive. Some in his entourage must have thought that this whole adventure was one big mistake. Had Abraham heard from God?

Once in Egypt, his people were to witness his humiliation as he surrendered his wife to Pharaoh to protect himself. Was this man worth following?

It was only after his return from Egypt that Abraham was finally shown his destination. Genesis 13:14-15:

> *"And the Lord said unto Abram, after that Lot was separated*
> *from him, Lift up now thine eyes, and look from the place*
> *where thou art northward, and southward, and eastward, and*
> *westward: For all the land which thou seest, to thee will I give*
> *it, and to thy seed forever".*

Parts of God's promise sounded highly improbable:
> *"...unto thy seed will I give this land."* (Genesis 12:7).

> *"And I will make thy seed as the dust of the earth: so that if a*

man can number the dust of the earth, then shall thy seed also be numbered." (Genesis 13:16).

What seed? The man was well into his seventies and still childless. His wife was an old woman past childbearing age. Yet Abraham followed God and led others on the basis of the highly improbable promise that God was going to make of him *"a great nation"* (Genesis 12:2).

According to Genesis 21:5, it took twenty-five **years** for him to see this particular part of the promise fulfilled:

"And Abraham was a hundred years old, when his son Isaac was born unto him."

Yet Abraham believed.

While it may be easier to see how we must respond to the "spiritual" causes of our times by faith, we often struggle to understand how the lessons of faith can be applied to leadership in general. The secular humanism of our times often forces us to distinguish spiritual leadership from the secular, and to keep an active and armed border guard between the two, promptly punishing any border jumpers and shooting down any attempts to blur the lines.

We run into problems, however, when we realize that the lines were extremely blurred in the case of Moses, David, Gideon, Deborah, Daniel, Joseph, et al. What we discover in studying the lives of these men and women is that their faith was very relevant to the solving of practical problems and accomplishing of tasks. They accomplished both "secular" and spiritual tasks by faith. Their faith was the reason they were so successful in accomplishing their leadership tasks. Joseph was a successful Prime Minister of Egypt because of his faith. Moses liberated the children of Israel from the bondage of Egypt and led them towards the Promised Land by faith. Along the way, he resolved many non-spiritual problems by faith.

When the children of Israel were hemmed in by a determined enemy on the one hand and the Red Sea on the other, one could hardly say that they were in a spiritual quandary. While their situation had spiritual implications, the challenge was certainly a non-spiritual one. Yet Moses did not fall back on a brilliant military strategy drawn up by brilliant subordinates to bring the children of Israel out. Instead he prayed in faith to the God of Israel for deliverance by the might of His hand.

The thirst of the children of Israel at Meribah was not a spiritual thirst or a spiritual problem. Yet instead of digging wells, Moses struck a rock in faith.

The flooded Jordan that Joshua and the children of Israel encountered as they journeyed to the land of promise was not a spiritual barrier. Yet they crossed by faith, not by boat. The fortifications at Jericho were not spiritual walls. Yet they succumbed to the shout and trump of faith of God's people.

The threat of the Midianites during Gideon's time was not a spiritual one. Yet God instructed Gideon to lead a faith army of 300 against an army of the Midianites and Amalekites described in the Scripture as being "like grasshoppers for multitude" (Judges 7:12). Deborah the prophetess and wife of Lapidoth was a successful judge and military commander in Israel on account of her faith.

Goliath and his Philistine army were not a spiritual threat to Israel. Yet David relied on the God of Israel to defeat the giant and the rest of the armies of the Philistines.

When we study the Bible, it seems we find that the most important weapon for leaders is faith. Faith invites God's helping hand into the efforts of men.   With it, we are virtually guaranteed success in everything we do. Hebrews 11:2 tells us that by faith the leaders of old obtained a good report. They were spoken well of and obtained high leadership marks because of the success they enjoyed from leading by faith.

The Bible also makes it clear that it takes one who is living and walking by faith to lead by faith.   These leaders did not borrow a few spiritual principles and apply them to the practice of leadership.

They believed in God!

They understood that the power of applying a spiritual principle can only be derived from believing its author. We couldn't imitate the exploits of these men and women of faith and expect any success without believing in God . We can hit all the rocks we want, but without faith in God, no water will come forth.

Hebrews 12:2 tells us that Jesus is the author and finisher of our faith. It is His expectation that we lead by an anointed and empowered faith. After laying a foundation of faith and obedience in the lives of His disciples, He pointed them to Pentecost (Luke 24:49) to put the tips on the arrows of their faith. His insistence that they needed to be endued with power at Pentecost shows us that He considered their faith to be unfinished until they had experienced the power anointing.

No less important was the fact that He did not give them the power anointing at the beginning of the discipleship process. There was a foundational process in the building of their faith that needed to precede the power anointing.   While the power anointing would have enabled the disciples to do dramatic things, it was more important for them to understand the need for faithful obedience to God's will.

Jesus is not interested in merely equipping us to take shortcuts to glory. He anoints our faith to enable us to accomplish God's purposes according to His will. When those who sought His life confronted Jesus, He did not use the anointing to defend Himself. That was not the purpose for which the anointing had been given. Similarly, many of His disciples died terrible deaths at the hands of their persecutors even though they could have used the anointing to save themselves.

Walking in faith to the step of God's will must take precedence over the use of the anointing. He does not finish our faith with His anointing so we can kill our enemies, but to advance God's will. Jesus makes it clear in John 14:30-31 that He submitted to death at the Cross not because He had no power over the devil, but in obedience to God:

> "...the ruler of this world is coming. He has no power over me;
> but I do as the Father has commanded me, so that the world
> may know that I love the Father." (NRSV)

He sought to instill the same understanding in His disciples that obedience must prevail over power, telling them in Luke 10:19-20:

> "Behold, I give unto you power to tread on serpents and
> scorpions, and over all the power of the enemy: and nothing
> shall by any means hurt you. Notwithstanding in this rejoice
> not, that the spirits are subject unto you; but rather rejoice,
> because your names are written in heaven."

The power anointing will not keep us from making foolish and dangerous decisions. It should not be considered a substitute for faith and obedience. Saul, the first king of Israel, stepped outside of faith and obedience and made some tragic decisions, his anointing notwithstanding. In 1 Samuel 10:6, the prophet Samuel had told the young king:

> *"...the Spirit of the LORD will come upon thee, and thou shalt prophesy with them, and shalt be turned into another man."*

When the prophet said Saul was going to be turned into another man, he did not mean that a deep transformation of character would result from the Spirit of the Lord coming upon him. All he meant was that Saul would prophesy at Gilgal.

According to 1 Samuel 10:10, he did prophesy with the company of the prophets at Gilgal, but still made the foolish decisions that cost him his kingdom and his life (1 Samuel 13/14/15). Prophesying at Gilgal was not necessarily a sign of a finished and deep faith, even though it was an impressive performance that did not go unnoticed:

> *"And it came to pass, when all that knew him beforetime saw that, behold, he prophesied among the prophets, then the people said one to another, What is this that is come unto the son of Kish? Is Saul also among the prophets?"* (1 Samuel 10:11).

It is also important to understand that the power anointing does not exempt us from the requirement to study God's word and to rightly divide it. Paul writes in his letter to his young protégé Timothy (2 Timothy 2:15):

> *"Study to shew thyself approved unto God, a workman that needeth not to be ashamed, rightly dividing the word of truth."*

The experience of Pentecost does not magically make us able to live according to the truth that we know. In Galatians 2:11-17 Paul confronted Peter, Barnabas and the others for walking in an anointed hypocrisy that was very harmful to the cause of Christ. Paul knew that Peter and Barnabas, and everyone else who had been *"carried away with their dissimulation…"* concerning the Gentiles, *"…walked not uprightly according to the truth of the gospel,"* not because they did not know the truth, or were not anointed, but because they made a conscious choice to not walk according to the truth.

Jesus wants us to have the kind of faith that understands that it is more important to know God's will before we jump into the fight, a faith that wields the sword of the Spirit, which is the word of God, as its weapon in our fight against the darkness of this world.

It is this kind of faith which pleases Him.

the CHALLENGE - > Applying faith
to Leadership

1. Discuss some contemporary challenges to applying faith to the solving of every day "non-spiritual" problems.

2. What is the relationship between the anointing and faith?

3. How was Abraham's response to God's call not just a personal walk of faith, but also a demonstration of leadership by faith?

Personal lessons learned from Chapter 15

1.	
2.	
3.	

"By faith the walls of Jericho came down."
- Hebrews 11:30

SIXTEEN

Following A Tough Act

*Now after the death of Moses
the servant of the Lord, it came to pass
that the Lord spake unto Joshua the son of Nun,
Moses' minister, saying, Moses My servant is dead;
now therefore arise, go over this Jordan,
thou, and all this people, unto the land
which I do give to them, even to the children of Israel.*

JOSHUA 1:1-2

One of my favorite preachers of all time was the Rev. John Osteen, the late founder of Houston's Lakewood Church. At the time of his death in 1999, the church had grown from a handful of worshippers in a converted feed store in 1959 to a 6,000 member church. The quintessential pastor, preacher, teacher and exhorter, John Osteen's message was a biblically sound, unforgettable, and uplifting message of hope that touched the lives of millions of people all over the world. Many wondered upon hearing of his death if anyone was going to be able to fill his shoes at Lakewood.

It was painful watching Joel Osteen's first few nervous moments as he took the pulpit to preach his first sermon following his father's death. Since then, Joel has developed a no less effective style of his own which has made him one of my favorite preachers. The church has experienced tremendous growth under his leadership, more than quadrupling its membership in five years to become at 25,000 plus members, the largest church in America.

What is the reason for Joel Osteen's success? He is succeeding because he is comfortable with the fact that God did not call him to be his father. Joel Osteen is no John Osteen, just as Joshua was no Moses and Elisha was no Elijah. Joel is succeeding by being Joel.

We put unbearable and unnecessary pressure on ourselves when we do not recognize that leadership shoes are cut to size. What God expects is for us to step into our own and walk confidently in them, even as we build upon the work of those who have gone before us and draw the lessons we must from their leadership method.

The story of Elijah and Elisha in the book of Kings provides some valuable lessons. Elijah, one of the greatest prophets in the history of Israel, a man who had resurrected the dead, commanded the heavens to withhold rain for three years, and prayed down fire from heaven, was no easy act for anyone to follow.

Upon finding out that he was the chosen successor, it was clear to Elisha that he had much to learn from the great prophet before he departed to glory. Immediately, Elisha abandoned everything to follow the prophet (1 Kings 19: 19-21). Notice that no one told Elisha to follow him. Elijah did not compel Elisha to submit to him as one of the requirements of succession. It was up to Elisha to recognize the difference sitting under Elijah would make to his ministry.

Not everyone God calls responds with the Elisha kind of humility. Satan is often quick to pour his witches' brew of pride and arrogance into the mix, causing the newly called to believe they are better than those they are being called to replace. Elisha knew better than to entertain any such foolishness from the devil and positioned himself to receive the training and impartation to improve his chances of success after Elijah's departure.

Even with all the training and impartation, Elisha's sense of inadequacy was still evident in his final request to the prophet:

> *"...I pray thee, let a double portion of thy spirit be upon me."* (2 Kings 2:9).

Some have suggested that Elisha was requesting the double-portion so he could outperform the old prophet. That does not seem to fit with what we know of Elisha's character. A more logical interpretation would be that he felt it would take a double portion of Elijah's anointing sitting on a nobody like himself to live up to the great prophet's accomplishments.

Even after the prophet had granted him his wish, Elisha still felt inadequate. Arriving at the banks of the river Jordan after witnessing Elijah being taken up to glory, he smote the waters, not expecting them to obey him as they had his departed master, uttering in frustration (2 Kings 2:14):

> *"Where is the Lord God of Elijah?"*

It took the sons of the prophets who saw the waters parting for him to recognize that *"...the spirit of Elijah doth rest on Elisha..."* (verse 15). Once he had crossed over, he agreed to send out a search party for the old prophet (verses 16-17). Whilst the Bible tells us that he was reluctant to send out the search party, from what we know of him Elisha would have most likely been greatly relieved had Elijah been found.

It was not long thereafter that Elisha settled into the uniqueness of his call. Recognizing that God was as committed to him as He had been to Elijah, he served faithfully and became one of the greatest prophets in Israel's history.

In an earlier time, no one would have faulted Joshua for being terrified at the prospect of succeeding a man about whom the Scriptures say:

> *"And there arose not a prophet since in Israel like unto Moses, whom the Lord knew face to face, in all the signs and the wonders, which the Lord sent him to do in the land of Egypt, to Pharaoh, and to all His servants, and to all His land, And in all that mighty hand, and in all the great terror, which Moses shewed in the sight of all Israel"* (Deuteronomy 34:10-12).

Fortunately like Elisha, Joshua had humbly sat at the feet of Moses and received the training necessary to fulfill the responsibilities of leadership. We also read in Deuteronomy 34:9 that he had received impartation through the laying on of hands:

> *"And Joshua the son of Nun was full of the spirit of wisdom; for Moses had laid his hands upon him: and the children of Israel hearkened unto him, and did as the Lord commanded Moses"*.

While the imprint of the great human hands through which we pass as we are molded will be evident in our lives, God calls us to a personal expression of His purpose. God promised to prosper Joshua's leadership in its own right if he observed God's law, not if he was a successful Moses impersonator (Joshua 1:8). God was as committed to Joshua's success as He had been to Moses':

> *"Every place that the sole of your foot shall tread upon, that I have given unto you, as I said unto Moses. From the wilderness*

and this Lebanon even unto the great river Euphrates, all the land of the Hittites, and unto the great sea toward the going down of the sun, shall be your coast. There shall not any man be able to stand before thee all the days of thy life: as I was with Moses, so I will be with thee: I will not fail thee, nor forsake thee." (Joshua 1:3-5).

When God calls us, we even inherit the promises made to the great leaders that precede us. The promises God made to Moses were not personal, but had something to do with the advancing of His kingdom. If they had been personal, they would have perished with Moses at Mt. Nebo. Instead the Lord told Joshua as He had told Moses before him:

"Every place that the sole of your foot shall tread upon, that I have given unto you, as I said unto Moses" (Joshua 1:3).

God does not make mistakes. He knew exactly whom He was calling when He called you, just as He knew when He was calling Moses that He was calling someone with a self-image problem. It is liberating to realize that those who become the great leaders of our times were yesterday's amateurs, quaking with fear at the greatness of the responsibilities God was committing into their hands.

It is important to know what to request from God in prayer when we are called to succeed great leaders. Young King Solomon, faced with succeeding his great father David, asked God to establish His promises to David and to grant him wisdom and knowledge to judge His people (2 Chronicles 1:7-12). Because he asked for the right thing, God granted his request and more, and Solomon's leadership became distinguished in its own right.

Ultimately, any leader, including a failure, is a tough act to follow if we operate under the misapprehension that we can succeed without relying on God. The best leadership manual one could ever have is the word of God. Remember the words of Psalm 1:

> *"Blessed is the man that walketh not in the counsel of the ungodly, nor standeth in the way of sinners, nor sitteth in the seat of the scornful. But his delight is in the law of the LORD; and in his law doth he meditate day and night. And he shall be like a tree planted by the rivers of water, that bringeth forth his fruit in his season; his leaf also shall not wither; and whatsoever he doeth shall prosper. The ungodly are not so: but are like the chaff which the wind driveth away. Therefore the ungodly shall not stand in the judgment, nor sinners in the congregation of the righteous. For the LORD knoweth the way of the righteous: but the way of the ungodly shall perish."*
> (Psalm 1:1-6).

the CHALLENGE - > **Trust His work in you**

1. Why was Joshua not intimidated by the success of his great predecessor?

2. What do you understand by the statement that leadership shoes are cut to size?

3. Why is succession not necessarily a repudiation of the old?

Personal lessons learned from Chapter 16

1.	
2.	
3.	

"I have called thee by thy name; thou art mine"
- Isaiah 43:1

SEVENTEEN

The Power Of One

*One man of you
shall chase a thousand:
for the Lord your God,
He it is that fighteth for you,
as He hath promised you.*

J O S H U A 23:10

*Behind every
dazzling leadership success
is the prophetic promise of God
for that particular outcome.*

God has an exasperating habit of calling one person where a thousand are needed. His call often looks more like a call to failure than to success.

Implicit in God's promise that one shall chase a thousand is the fact that we are almost always called to a position of disadvantage. Moses was called to a monumental challenge. For the children of Israel, going against Pharaoh was unthinkable. Moses' arrival from Midian did not change their numbers in any significant way. They were still hopelessly outnumbered. Egypt still had a vast army and sufficient resources to continue oppressing the Hebrews for many more years.

Moses had no great plan and no great weapon. By his own admission, he had no confidence in his ability to move Israel to revolution:

> *"And Moses said unto God, who am I, that I should go unto Pharaoh, and that I should bring forth the children of Israel out of Egypt?"* (Exodus 3:11).

Moses knew that it was not seeing the burning bush that really counted, but the Lord's involvement and commitment to the success of the mission. The Scripture promises that one shall chase a thousand because

> *"...the Lord your God, He it is that fighteth for you, as He hath promised you."* (Joshua 23:10).

Deuteronomy 32:30 also tells us that one shall chase a thousand because God shall abandon the enemy, thereby undermining his strength:

> *"How should one chase a thousand, and two put ten thousand to flight, except their Rock had sold them, and the Lord had shut them up?"*

In addition to the Lord's involvement and commitment to his success, Moses was faithful and committed to what He had been called. Moses triumphed against great odds because he pursued the purpose of his encounter with God. He would have failed miserably if, after his encounter, he had sought to evangelize Midian. That was neither the purpose of his encounter nor the outcome to which God was committed.

What God was committed to was freeing His people from Egyptian bondage (Exodus 3:7-8).

"And the Lord said, I have surely seen the affliction of My people which are in Egypt, and have heard their cry by reason of their taskmasters: for I know their sorrows; and I am come down to deliver them out of the hand of the Egyptians..."

This was an assignment Moses was in no position to lose, no matter how bad the odds. God was obligated to victory for His people Israel at this particular moment in history. It did not matter that they were few. It did not matter that they did not have weaponry. It did not matter that they did not have a vast army. Victory was guaranteed.

Behind every dazzling and supernatural leadership success is the prophetic promise of God for that particular outcome, and His direct involvement in the activity leading to it. Indeed, it is His commitment to His promise and His involvement that creates great leaders.

God's great force multipliers are people who walk in obedience and know and trust the God method.

In Judges 7, an army of three hundred Hebrews under Gideon's leadership prevailed against a vast coalition of several thousand Midianites and Amalekites. When the Lord told him to trim his army of thirty-two thousand down to three hundred men, Gideon obeyed even though it did not make any sense. His obedience proved to be greater than the thirty-one thousand seven hundred armed men God told him to leave behind.

When the armies of Israel and the Philistines squared off in the valley of Elah the ability of the children of Israel to prevail over the Philistines increased dramatically with the addition of a little shepherd boy. The boy David had neither military training nor a super-weapon to offer Saul's army. When David offered to go against the Philistine behemoth, King Saul thought it was preposterous (1 Samuel 17:33):

> "...thou art not able to go against this Philistine to fight with him: for thou art but a youth, and he a man of war from his youth."

David was a discouraging sight as he struggled and failed to walk in the armor that Saul provided him. In addition to the ill-fitting armor, the sword felt and looked awkward in his grasp.

David's next actions would have been amusing had the circumstances not been terribly serious. After removing the armor and putting down the sword, he

> "...took his staff in his hand, and chose him five smooth stones out of the brook, and put them in a shepherd's bag which he had, even in a scrip, and his sling was in his hand: and he drew near to the Philistine." (1 Samuel 17:40).

But then, had Samson not slain a thousand men with the jawbone of an ass (Judges 15:15)?

David did not bring more of what Israel perceived she lacked onto the battlefield. He was neither a bigger giant than Goliath, nor more experienced at handling the instruments of war.

What made the balance swing in Israel's favor was the fact that David came in the power of God's name and not in the pride of experience, training and technology:

"Then said David to the Philistine, Thou comest to me with a sword, and with a spear, and with a shield: but I come to thee in the name of the Lord of hosts, the God of the armies of Israel, whom thou hast defied." (1 Samuel 17:45).

He knew whom he represented. His trust rested not in the carnal weapons fashioned by men (*"And all this assembly shall know that the Lord saveth not with sword and spear..."* I Samuel 17:47) but in the Lord in whose cause he stood.

He understood that this was not about him and that the Lord whom this Philistine had defied would vindicate Himself in this battle (1 Samuel 17:37).

As he had acknowledged and carried the presence of the Lord into his fight against the lion and the bear (*"The Lord that delivered me out of the paw of the Lion, and out of the paw of the bear..."*), he carried the same presence and anointing into the current battle (*He will deliver me out of the hand of this Philistine"* I Samuel 17:37).

It was that same anointing that had caused Samson, and other great men, to do tremendous exploits before David's time (Judges 14:5-6):

> *"...a young lion roared against him. And the Spirit of the Lord came mightily upon him (Samson), and he rent him as he would have rent a kid, and he had nothing in his hand."*

Leaders who become great force-multipliers are, like David, able to put their testimonies to effective use. They understand that the victories from past partnerships with God are serious weapons that must be deployed in the present day battle.

What makes our past testimonies relevant to today's battles is not so much the similarity of the battles. Facing Goliath and the Philistines was not the same as facing the lion and the bear. What was relevant was not the method but The Helper. Past testimonies become relevant to today's challenges because they attest to God's ability. When we invoke a past testimony in battle, we are bringing the proven ability of God to the current situation.

It is easy to present the great force multipliers of the Scriptures as superheroes who could do it all by themselves and who needed no help from men. What we discover from the Scriptures, however, is that an important part of leadership is knowing when to ask for help, and when to stop hiding our need from those God has sent to help us.

God sent *"helpers of the war"* to David when he was in the wilderness fleeing from Saul (1 Chronicles 12:1). He would have been foolish not to utilize these men whose mission according to 1 Chronicles 12: 23 was to "turn the kingdom of Saul to him, according to the word of the Lord". David accepted their help because he understood that it was not a sign of weakness to receive the help of a helper sent from God.

Moses was a great deliverer but an inefficient administrator who took too much upon himself. He was unable to see how much of a load he was carrying until his father-in-law Jethro pointed it out to him. During a visit with Moses in the wilderness of Mt. Sinai, Jethro was disturbed by Moses' leadership method. Moses would sit all day resolving every dispute and presiding over every case the people brought to him as the rest of the congregation of Israel stood all day waiting their turn. Convinced that this was an unsustainable situation, Jethro confronted Moses, telling the great leader in Exodus 18:18:

"Thou wilt surely wear away, both thou, and this people that is with thee: for this thing is too heavy for thee; thou art not able to perform it thyself alone."

Moses humbled himself and implemented Jethro's counsel and appointed leaders to share the workload.

Peter the disciple of Christ, certainly knew when to cry out for help. When he got out of the boat in the middle of the sea to walk on the water towards Jesus, we read in Matthew 14:30-31 that

"when he saw the wind boisterous, he was afraid; and beginning to sink, he cried, saying, Lord, save me. And immediately Jesus stretched forth his hand, and caught him, and said unto him, O thou of little faith, wherefore didst thou doubt?" (Matthew 14: 31-32).

We can focus so much on Peter's rashness and Jesus' rebuke for his faithlessness and miss an equally important lesson here: what to do when we find ourselves in the middle of our Peter moments. While Peter's lack of confidence that he could stay afloat in the presence of the Lord was a sign of faithlessness, calling out to Jesus for help was a sign of faith in the Lord. While we may start sinking because of faithlessness, we must cry out to Him for help even if what we are asking Him to pull us out of is the product of our faithlessness.

It will not always be the Lord who will be in a position to help us. Help may appear in the form of a person Jesus sends. It is foolishness to dismiss the outstretched human hands of a God-sent helper simply because they are not nail scarred. We are not less spiritual because we receive the help of men.

Peter knew that it was more important to live than to worry that the others in the boat might think he was a coward. He knew that it was better to cry for help before he was in over his head.

Even the greatest leaders get overwhelmed. When you know when to call for help, you will live to fight another day.

the CHALLENGE - > Believe God, not the odds

1. What makes a testimony a force-multiplier?

2. How does the fact that the battle belongs to God help us succeed when the odds are heavily against us?

3. Why is it important to know one's limits?

Personal lessons learned from Chapter 17

1.
2.
3.

"With God all things are possible."
- Matthew 19:26

EIGHTEEN

The Purpose Of
Your Wilderness

*And Jesus being
full of the Holy Ghost
returned from Jordan,
and was led by the Spirit
into the wilderness.*

LUKE 4:1.

*The wilderness experience
is as much for the
obedient and humble
as it is for the Nebuchadnezzars
of this world.*

The word *wilderness* evokes images of wild, dangerous and scary places inhabited by wild beasts but inhospitable to normal human beings. The wilderness is a place of unease, physically, spiritually, and psychologically removed from where we believe God's purposes for our lives must unfold or be fulfilled. It is a place we believe people are driven to by Satan (Luke 8:29) and certainly not the place we were anointed to be in.

It is much easier to understand the purpose of the wilderness experience for the disobedient and proud. The Babylonian King Nebuchadnezzar's experience in Daniel 4 was designed to make him understand that God was jealous for His glory. Nebuchadnezzar had become so puffed up that walking in his palace one day he had declared:

> *"Is not this great Babylon, that I have built for the house of the kingdom by the might of my power, and for the honor of my majesty?"* (verse 30).

He immediately became insane and was driven from his palace to live like a beast in the wilderness. After seven years of eating grass "as oxen" and being at the mercy of the elements "till his hairs were grown like eagles' feathers, and his nails like birds' claws" (verse 33), he looked up to heaven and his understanding returned to him. The humiliation brought him to a place of acknowledging God (verses 34-37).

The uncomfortable reality the Bible confronts us with is that the wilderness experience is as much for the obedient and humble as it is for the Nebuchadnezzars of this world. We read in Hebrews 11: 36-38 concerning God's faithful servants:

> *"And others had trial of cruel mockings and scourgings, yea, moreover of bonds and imprisonment; they were stoned, they were sawn asunder, were tempted, were slain with the sword: they wandered about in sheepskins and goatskins; being destitute, afflicted, tormented; (of whom the world was not worthy:) they wandered in deserts and in mountains, and in dens and caves of the earth."*

After being anointed king by the prophet Samuel, David spent several years in the wilderness running away from King Saul. Elijah practically lived in the wilderness because of his uncompromising stand for righteousness in the face of King Ahab's wickedness.

For some of God's choice servants the journey of leadership starts in the wilderness, goes out of it and returns through it as they press faithfully towards the promised end. Moses received his call in the wilderness (Exodus 3), and passing through it on his way from Egypt to the Promised Land, he was equipped with the "lively oracles" (Acts 7:38) that became the guiding principles of his leadership.

The wilderness is a place where God's purpose in us is tested and strengthened. For John the Baptist (Luke 3:2), the apostle Paul (Galatians 1:17) and Jesus (Luke 4:1), it was a finishing school where God Himself crossed the Ts and dotted the Is of great ministries about to unfold.

The wilderness is a place where He proves His sufficiency. It is a place where our needs are exposed and His providence is provoked. Elijah's flight from Ahab and Jezebel exposed his need, to which the Lord responded with meals-on-wings (1 Kings 17: 2-6).

The psalmist writes that during their wilderness experience, the children of Israel murmured against God (Psalm 78:19), questioning whether He could "furnish a table in the wilderness". According to Nehemiah 9:19-21, He did more than that:

> *"Yet Thou in Thy manifold mercies forsookest them not in the wilderness: the pillar of the cloud departed not from them by day, to lead them in the way; neither the pillar of fire by night, to show them light, and the way wherein they should go. Thou gavest also Thy good Spirit to instruct them, and withheldest*

> *not Thy manna from their mouth, and gavest them water for*
> *their thirst. Yea, forty years didst Thou sustain them in the*
> *wilderness, so that they lacked nothing; their clothes waxed not*
> *old, and their feet swelled not".*

Satan works overtime to convince us during our wilderness experiences that we have been forsaken by God and have lost our way. The children of Israel were neither forsaken nor lost. He responded to their need with appropriate provision. They ate their fill and experienced His faithful presence throughout their journey. His glory cloud and the pillar of fire were present to lead them in the way by day and by night.

Often His illumination will be just sufficient for us to see the few steps we need to take in the present. Even this is for our own good as it forces us to rely on Him and to walk in His ordering of our steps.

While we may think of the wilderness as a place of vulnerability, we see from the life of David that it can be a place of safety, a place beyond the reach of our enemies:

> *"And David abode in the wilderness in strongholds, and*
> *remained in a mountain in the wilderness of Ziph, And Saul*
> *sought him everyday, but God delivered him not into his hand".*
> (1 Samuel 23:14).

For the woman of Revelation 12 it was a place of safety prepared by God, a place the beast that was trying to devour the child she had just delivered could not reach. It was also a place for her sustenance (verse 6).

God prepares for us the least likely places for our refuge and nourishment. The important thing is not what we think of the place, but rather what God does when we are in it. It was more important for David to be safe than to be comfortable.

The Lord will give us the ability to flee into the wilderness when what we think we need is the ability to fight. The woman of Revelation 12:14 was given *"...two wings of a great eagle, that she might fly into the wilderness, into her place, where she is nourished for a time, and times, and half a time, from the face of the serpent"*. God could have given her the power to prevail over the dragon, but that was not His plan. Instead He chose for her to hide. We naturally don't think of hiding as a posture of leadership. Yet when we retreat to our places of refuge, not out of fear of the enemy but out of obedience to God, He is just as pleased as when we are charging forward to conquer and vanquish in obedience to His command.

We also see from the life of David that the wilderness is a place for the "helpers of the war" to come to our cause:

> *"Now these are they that came to David to Ziklag, while he yet kept himself close because of Saul the son of Kish: and they were among the mighty men, helpers of the war"*.
> (1 Chronicles 12:1)

The purpose of David's wilderness was to surround him with a circle of quality people who truly knew God's will. Those who came to David in Hebron did not come to his success, but to his cause. They did not come to his greatness but to fulfill God's word, to *"turn the kingdom of Saul to him, according to the word of the Lord"*. We worry about looking unsuccessful and un-leader like in our wilderness, yet ultimately what is important is being in the will of God, no matter how that may make us look. When we are in God's will, the "helpers of the war" will come to our aid even in our wilderness.

They came to David in droves *"until it was a great host, like the host of God"* (verse 22), the best fighting men in the armies of Israel. They were men who were *"fit for the battle, that could handle shield and buckler, whose faces were like the faces of lions, and were as swift as the roes upon the mountains"* (verse 8).

They were *"ready armed to the war"* (verse 23) to help fulfill God's purpose for David's life. They were a disciplined force, *"men of war, that could keep rank"* who came *"with a perfect heart to Hebron, to make David king over all Israel"* (verse 38).

They did not come when David wanted them to come, but they came in God's timing. Among them were men who had a clear understanding of God's will, *"the children of Isacchar, which were men that had understanding of the times, to know what Israel ought to do"* (verse 32). David was not just surrounded by men of brute force, but also by men of wisdom and knowledge who were led by the Spirit of God.

According to the word of God, the wilderness can also be a place of revival:

> *"Then shall the lame man leap as a hart, and the tongue of the dumb sing: for in the wilderness shall waters break out, and streams in the desert."* (Isaiah 35: 6).

While the wilderness is often the last place we expect to discover God's quickening presence, the reality is that God does not limit His presence to our comfort zones. In the 139th Psalm, David tells us that it is impossible to flee from the Lord's presence (verses 7-12). Our failure to discern the presence of the Lord does not mean that He is absent. Those who are able to discern His presence in the wilderness experience dramatic personal revivals and emerge renewed and ready for the fight.

the CHALLENGE - ⟩ Discovering the 🏔
purpose of your
wilderness

1. What do the wilderness experiences of the great leaders in the Scriptures tell us about their faith?

2. How can one be in God's will and in the wilderness at the same time?

3. If those who respond to God's call often find themselves in wildernesses, how is the call of God a blessing?

Personal lessons learned from Chapter 18

1.
2.
3.

"Can God furnish a table in the wilderness?"
- Psalm 78:19

NINETEEN

The School Of Betrayal

And ye shall be betrayed…

L U K E 21:16

*Have I not
chosen you twelve,
and one of you is a devil?*

J O H N 6:70

"This is the conclusion I have come to," a friend summed up our conversation. "Not only are we going to be betrayed, but we must be betrayed."

It is easy to stumble over any suggestion of the necessity of betrayal. While we may conclude from a specific experience of betrayal that we are better people for having gone through it, the idea of betrayal as a necessity may be too radical to accept for those whose lives have been traumatized by it.

No sane person enjoys being betrayed. We don't pray that we would be betrayed so that we can become better people. We all wish to never experience betrayal. We learn however from the life of Christ that there is betrayal that comes with the mission of leadership, and that the treachery of others can be our stepping-stone to glory.

Jesus had to be betrayed in order for Him to fulfill His Messianic mission. We must put Judas' treachery into perspective, recognizing that what seemed like a tragic episode in the ministry of Christ was not the end of the story. While the immediate consequences of the betrayal were unpleasant (*"the Son of Man shall be betrayed unto the chief priests and unto the scribes, and they shall condemn Him to death, And shall deliver Him to the Gentiles to mock, and to scourge, and to crucify Him:"*), God's purpose ultimately triumphed (*"He was buried, and... He rose again the third day according to the scriptures:"* 1 Corinthians 15:4)!

While a case can be made that we set ourselves up for betrayal through the choices of friends that we make, it is important to remember that Jesus was betrayed by someone who He had chosen Himself:

> *"Have not I chosen you twelve, and one of you*
> *is a devil?"* (John 6:70)

Judas was chosen by one whose judgment was without compare. Besides, betrayal will not only come through those we choose to associate with. According to Luke 21:16-19, in the end times it shall come from much closer to home:

> *"And ye shall be betrayed both by parents, and brethren, and kinsfolks, and friends; and some of you shall they cause to be put to death. And ye shall be hated of all men for My name's sake. But there shall not an hair of your head perish. In your patience possess ye your souls."*

Betrayal comes with the times and in spite of our good judgment. 2 Timothy 3:1-4 paints a picture of the last days as fertile ground for betrayal:

> *"This know also, that in the last days perilous times shall come. For men shall be lovers of their own selves, covetous, boasters, proud, blasphemers, disobedient to parents, unthankful, unholy, without natural affection, trucebreakers, false accusers, incontinent, fierce, despisers of those that are good, traitors, heady, highminded, lovers of pleasures more than lovers of God".*

It will test everything we think we know about people and about ourselves. Its very definition precludes our enemies being responsible for it. We fully expect our enemies to do us harm. It would be foolish to be disappointed when they do. We are betrayed by those we expect to love us, those from whom we expect loyalty - our parents, brothers, spouses, relatives, and yes, the friends that we choose for ourselves.

Interestingly, Jesus did not discover just before His betrayal at Gethsemane that Judas was a traitor. He knew it from the beginning according to John 6:64

> *"Jesus knew from the beginning who they were that believed not, and who should betray Him".*

Yet He continued to function with purpose, even including Judas in important ministry assignments. In Matthew 10 when He sent forth the twelve on a ministry tour, Judas was, along with everybody else, anointed for the mission:

> *"And when He had called unto Him His twelve disciples, He gave them power against unclean spirits, to cast them out, and*

to heal all manner of sickness and all manner of disease."
(Matthew 10:1-4).

Jesus had clearly discerned the purpose of His Judas. He understood that the agent of betrayal would have his own case to answer before God (*"woe unto that man by whom he is betrayed..."* Luke 22:22), and that the betrayal had been scripted into His journey by the Father Himself (*"And truly the Son of Man goeth, as it was determined"*). He would neither interfere with the process by which the Father had determined to advance His steps nor take the betrayal personally since it was not about Him, but about the mission.

He refused to react in destructive anger to the indifference of the disciples when in response to their insistence that He tell them who the traitor was, He revealed that it was Judas:

> *"He it is, to whom I shall give a sop, when I have dipped it. And when He had dipped the sop, He gave it to Judas Iscariot, the son of Simon"* (John 13:26).

When He turned to Judas and said to him:

> *"That thou doest, do quickly"* (verse 27).

they reacted with the convenient confusion of those who do not want to believe the truth:

> *"Now no man at the table knew for what intent He spake this unto him. For some of them thought, because Judas had the bag, that Jesus had said unto him, Buy those things that we have need of against the feast; or, that he should give something to the poor.* (verse 28-29)

After receiving the sop, Judas got up and slipped into the night.

The reaction of the disciples suggests that they either did not believe Jesus or thought He deserved the betrayal. Not even the zealous Peter jumped up to grab Judas by the throat to demand an explanation. Where was their outrage? Where was the righteous indignation? No one said anything to Judas. Instead they allowed him to slip into the night to continue on his path to perdition.

Jesus would have been justified to believe that their loyalty to one another had blinded them to the true nature of Judas' heart. After all, some of them had even murmured with Judas in Bethany when Mary the sister of Lazarus had anointed Jesus with a pound of expensive spikenard ointment. While we are told that Judas murmured because he was a thief (John 12:6), according to Mark 14:4-5 he was not the only one who did:

> *"And there were **some** that had indignation within **themselves**, and said, Why was this waste of the ointment made? For it might have been sold for more than three hundred pence, and have been given to the poor. And they murmured against her."*
> (Emphasis added)

There seems to have been some shared concerns about aspects of Jesus' leadership. It could very well be that some of them believed that Jesus was being a little paranoid concerning Judas.

Even as Jesus was speaking to them about Judas, the disciples were engaged in an inappropriate squabble over who was going to have the highest rank after Jesus was gone!

> *"and there was also a strife among them, which of them should*

be accounted the greatest." (Luke 22:24).

Afterwards, all Jesus got from the eleven were empty declarations of loyalty which were backed by neither deed nor passion:

> *"Though I should die with Thee, yet will I not deny Thee.*
> *Likewise also said all the disciples."* (Matthew 26:35).

If these disciples could not take a clear and unequivocal stand against Judas, where were they going to get the courage to stand against the killers who were determined to crucify Jesus? Jesus, understanding the purpose of His Judas and knowing that ultimate vindication came from God, did not react to them in anger, choosing instead to let the story unfold as the Lord directed it. Afterwards, it becomes clear that He won their eternal loyalty and devotion through His willingness to face it all alone.

After unmasking Judas, Jesus took the rest of His disciples to a place called Gethsemane. His pain and isolation were evident at Gethsemane. If there was ever a time when He needed the supportive presence of His disciples, it was then. Yet His obvious distress and request that they watch and pray with Him was met with indifference:

> *"And He cometh unto the disciples, and findeth them asleep,*
> *and saith unto Peter, What, could ye not watch with Me one*
> *hour?"* (Matthew 26:40).

Judas' active betrayal and the indifference of the eleven (which was in itself a form of betrayal) worked together to complete Jesus' isolation at Gethsemane. We hear Him crying out in agony by Himself as His disciples slept:

"...O My Father, if it is possible, let this cup pass from Me: nevertheless, not as I will, but as Thou wilt" (Matthew 26:39).

"...O my Father, if this cup may not pass away from Me, except I drink it, Thy will be done" (Matthew 26:42).

The journey of leadership invariably passes through the garden of Gethsemane. Betrayal drives us reluctantly to this test center. Everything that is human rebels against the agony and pain of Gethsemane, yet that is the place where we must allow God's will to prevail over our flesh. It is the place where, ultimately, purpose triumphs over pain.

It is also the place where those who were reluctant to act in our defense before, now act with belated zeal. We learn at Gethsemane that other people do not necessarily operate in the timing demanded by our emotional need. When Judas led the arresting party to Jesus, the other disciples were suddenly possessed of a warrior spirit:

"When they which were about Him saw what would follow, they said unto Him, Lord shall we smite with the sword? And one of them smote the servant of the high priest, and cut off his right ear" (Luke 22:49-50).

Such belated zeal provides very little comfort, coming as it often does when it is too late to make much of a difference. It angers the best of us as much as the belated repentance of our "Judases" which seems to always come too late to save us the pain (Matthew 27:3).

Gethsemane is the place of final acceptance of God's purpose for our lives. It is the place where we cross the line of no return. While Jesus had ministered effectively in the three years of His earthly ministry, rejecting Gethsemane would have ensured that He did not fulfill the purpose of His call.   While it was good that He had healed the sick and cast out devils, the purpose of His mission was to die at the cross of Calvary.   It was His commitment to that which was tested at Gethsemane.

There are many things the Lord will allow us to do before He brings us to the line of no return.   Many will build ministries that are successful according to the standards of the world before being brought to the line of no return where they must commit to the true purpose of their callings.   Most of what the Lord will allow us to do before our Gethsemane is nothing but a pointer to God's purpose and a progression towards it.

Unfortunately, we can become so trapped by the pointers that we forego the purpose.   Why would a minister as successful as Jesus choose to accept the assignment to die instead of enjoying being the head of this dynamic ministry?   The challenge is to come to the line and to cross it willingly… to drink the cup and see the purpose of our callings being fulfilled.

the CHALLENGE - > Learning through your pain

1. What do we learn from the life of Christ about how to deal with betrayal?

2. How important is adversity to the fulfillment of God's purpose for our lives?

3. To what extent are we responsible for the betrayal that we experience?

Personal lessons learned from Chapter 19

1.

2.

3.

"O my Father, if it is possible, let this cup pass from me: nevertheless, not as I will, but as thou wilt."

- Matthew 26:39

TWENTY

Others May!
You Cannot!

*Moses forfeited the right
to enter the Promised Land
by simply striking the rock twice
in anger at Meribah-Kadesh.
Others have gotten away
with much worse.*

Many of us have a difficult time when God expects us to meet standards He does not expect of others. Wishing that He would treat us the same way He treats everybody else, we protest forcefully when He singles us out for extra effort and extra obedience.

In an article published by the Union Gospel Press of Ohio titled "Others May! You Cannot!" the anonymous author argues that it is the Lord's prerogative to deal individually with each person that He calls, placing upon each one of us unique demands of obedience:

> *If God has called you to be really like Jesus, He will draw you into a life of crucifixion and humility and put upon you demands of obedience. You will not be able to follow other people or measure yourself by other Christians, for in many ways He will seem to let other good people do things which He will not let you do.*

Other Christians and ministers, who seem very religious and useful, may push themselves, pull strings, and work schemes to carry out their plans, but you cannot do it. If you attempt it, you will meet with such failure and rebuke from the Lord as to make you sorely penitent.

Others may boast of themselves, of their work, of their successes, of their writings; but the Holy Spirit will not allow you to do any such thing. If you begin it, He will lead you into some deep mortification that will make you despise yourself and all your good works.

Others may succeed in earning money, or may have legacies left to them; but it is likely God will keep you poor because He wants you to have something far better than gold – namely, a helpless dependence upon Him so that He may have the privilege of supplying your needs from an unseen treasury day by day.

The Lord may let others be honored and noticed, but keep you hidden in obscurity because He wants to produce some choice, fragrant fruit for His coming glory which can be produced only in the shade. He may let others do a work for Him and get the credit for it; but He will make you work and toil, without your knowing how much you are doing. Then to make your work still more precious, He may let others get credit for the work you have done, thus making your reward ten times greater when Jesus comes.

The Holy Spirit will put a strict watch over you, with a jealous love, and will rebuke you for little words and feelings, or for wasting time, things over which other Christians never feel distressed. So make up your mind that God is an Omnipotent Sovereign and has a right to do as He pleases with His own. He may not explain to you a thousand things which puzzle your reason in His dealings with you; but if you absolutely give yourself to Him, He will wrap you up in a jealous love and bestow upon you many blessings which come only to those who are in the inner circle.

Settle it forever, then, that you are to deal directly with the Holy Spirit and that He is to have the privilege of tying your tongue, chaining your hand, or closing your eyes in ways that He does not seem to use with others. Now, when you are so possessed with the living God that you are, in your secret heart, pleased and delighted over this peculiar, personal, private, jealous guardianship and management of the Holy Spirit over your life, you will have found the entrance to heaven.

(Reprinted by permission of The Incorporated Trustees of the Gospel Works Society, Union Gospel Press P.O. Box 6059, Cleveland Ohio 44101).

God sets different standards for different people because He calls different people to different calls. Clearly, He expects all of us to fear Him and to obey all His commandments (Ecclesiastes 12:13-14). He expects us all to be without sin (2 Peter 3:14), to seek the kingdom and His righteousness before all else (Matthew 6:32-33), to love one another (John 13:34-35) etc. We all understand and largely accept that the general requirements of the faith apply to all of us.

Beyond that however, it is important to recognize that God has the right to define the standards to which He will hold each individual He calls. The uniqueness of the standards derives from what He wants to accomplish with each individual He chooses.

We all enter into different "contracts" with God. Each "contract" is unique and specific. When He called Israel, He called her specifically:

"I have called thee by thy name; thou art Mine". (Isaiah 43:1).

In addition to the contract with Israel being specific, He called her to belong to Him, telling her: "thou art Mine". God had every right to require of Israel what He did not require of others because of the uniqueness of Israel's call, and in exercise of His prerogative of ownership.

The contract with Moses was equally unique. No one else except Moses had the burning bush experience (Exodus 3). When we understand this, it becomes easier to deal with the fact that someone else striking the rock twice at Meribah-Kadesh might have received a less drastic punishment than what Moses received. The reason why a seemingly minor infraction cost Moses the right to enter the Promised Land (Deuteronomy 32:48-52) had everything to do with the unique demands of obedience his contract with God placed on him.

Saul lost his kingdom for taking the initiative to offer the burnt offering to God when the prophet Samuel was late in coming to perform his priestly duties. According to 1 Samuel 13:13-14, by failing to keep the commandment that the Lord had commanded him, the king was in breach of contract. We stand logic on its head when we complain about God's expectation that we live up to the standards specific to our callings while demanding higher bracket rewards.

In addition to observing the specific commandments He gives us, the Lord expects us to yield to the day to day "guardianship and management" of our lives by the Holy Spirit. While such micromanagement may cramp the style of the lawless, we see from the Scriptures that it was responsible for the success of the great servants of God. They did not go to war without His leading. They ruled the nations under His direction. They spread the news of the Gospel and did exploits under His leadership.

Paul, Silas and Timothy were clearly yielded to His minute-by-minute, play-by-play leading. In Acts 16:6-10, they were headed to Asia to preach when the Holy Spirit forbade them to go. They turned, and passing through Mysia were going to proceed to Bithynia when the Spirit of God interdicted them again.

When they came to Troas, Paul had a vision that directed them to Macedonia:

> *"And a vision appeared to Paul in the night: there stood a man of Macedonia, and prayed him, saying, Come over into Macedonia, and help us. And after he had seen the vision, immediately we endeavoured to go into Macedonia, assuredly gathering that the Lord had called us for to preach the gospel unto them."* (Acts 16:9-10).

They could have insisted on going to Asia and Bithynia on the grounds that there were sinners there also who needed to hear the word. These men were all self-starting go-getters who were zealous in seeking out opportunities to do good. At the same time, they understood that it was more important to submit to God's will than to insist on pursuing their own agenda.

When we submit to the Holy Spirit's guardianship, He will jealously guard what we do, our relationships, where we go etc. In Elijah's case, He jealously guarded the prophet's loneliness, not giving him much room to enjoy the companionship of others. Like any normal human being, Elijah had his moments of frustration when he struggled to understand why the Lord placed such strict requirements on him. When he complained in 1 Kings 19:10 that he was the only one left who was serving the Lord with zeal, the Lord corrected him, telling him that there were seven thousand others *"in Israel, all the knees which have not bowed unto Baal, and every mouth which hath not kissed him"* (1 Kings 19:18) Why had Elijah concluded that he was the only one serving the Lord with zeal? Because he did not see the Lord requiring others to walk and fight alone as He required of him.

God never told Elijah what His requirements of the seven thousand prophets were. It had nothing to do with Elijah. It would not have helped Elijah in any way to try and compare his "conditions of service" with those of the others God called. What he needed to focus on were God's expectations of him as an individual so that he could work on his own obedience.

In addition to individual compliance with His expectations, God is pleased when we set high standards of righteousness for ourselves. He was pleased when Daniel and his friends purposed in their hearts not to defile themselves with King Nebuchadnezzar's meat nor with the wine which he drank, preferring pulse for their daily rations (Daniel 1: 8-16). He rewarded the young men with *"knowledge and skill in all learning and wisdom"* and Daniel with *"understanding in all visions and dreams"* (verse 17).

Because they understood the importance of the ministries to which they had been called, they did not waste time complaining about how tough life in exile was. Instead they set higher standards for themselves. When the challenges came, God who was clearly pleased with their commitment to higher standards rescued them from the wrath of the king (Daniel 2:1-13), the mouth of the lions (Daniel 6) and the fiery furnace (Daniel 3). As a result of their commitment to higher standards, the king of Babylon and the whole of his pagan kingdom witnessed tremendous testimonies of who God was, leading Nebuchadnezzar to fall upon his face and declare:

> "...Of a truth it is, that your God is a God of gods, and a Lord of kings..." (Daniel 2:47).

> "...Blessed be the God of Shadrach, Meshach, and Abednego, who hath sent his angel, and delivered his servants that trusted in him, and have changed the king's word, and yielded their bodies, that they might not serve nor worship any god, except their own God. Therefore I make a decree, That every people, nation, and language, which speak any thing amiss against the God of Shadrach, Meshach, and Abednego, shall be cut in pieces, and their houses shall be made a dunghill: because there is no other God that can deliver after this sort" (Daniel 3:28-29).

Daniel and his friends were to similarly impress Nebuchadnezzar's successors, including King Darius, who seeing their faith, also declared in Daniel 6: 26-27:

> "I make a decree, That in every dominion of my kingdom men tremble and fear before the God of Daniel: for he is the living God, and stedfast for ever, and his kingdom that which shall not be destroyed, and his dominion shall be even unto the end. He delivereth and rescueth, and he worketh signs and wonders in heaven and in earth, who hath delivered Daniel from the power of the lions."

Like Daniel and his friends in Babylon, when we live up to the high standards that He sets for us, and the higher standards we set ourselves, we allow the light of His glory to shine into our Babylon for the advancement of the kingdom.

the CHALLENGE -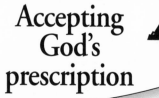

Accepting God's prescription

1. What are some of the unique demands of obedience God has placed on your life and how have you dealt with them?

2. Is it possible to do great things for the kingdom in obscurity?

3. If God judges individuals according to His expectation of them, does that mean there are no absolutes in the kingdom? What challenges does that present to defining sin?

Personal lessons learned from Chapter 20

1.	
2.	
3.	

"God reserves the right to single you out for extra effort and extra obedience."

- Author

TWENTY ONE

Raising the Bar

*"If thou hast run with the footmen,
and they have wearied thee,
then how canst thou contend with horses?"*

JEREMIAH 12:5

*A leader's definition of crisis
must be different from that
of the people he leads.*

The prophet Jeremiah was unhappy and clearly in the middle of an Asaph moment (see Psalm 73). Observing the prosperity and merriment of the wicked, he was troubled by how God's favor could prefer the wicked over His own. Weary and confused, he demanded an explanation:

> *"Righteous art thou, O LORD, when I plead with thee: yet let
> me talk with thee of thy judgments: Wherefore doth the way of
> the wicked prosper? wherefore are all they happy that deal very
> treacherously? Thou hast planted them, yea, they have taken
> root: they grow, yea, they bring forth fruit: thou art near in their
> mouth, and far from their reins"* (Jeremiah 12:1-2).

Clearly disappointed that the prophet had allowed himself to be wearied by envy, God reminded him that he had been called to a much higher standard of leadership. In essence, what God was saying was that Jeremiah's despondency was a direct result of the prophet lowering the bar:

> *"If thou hast run with the footmen, and they have wearied thee, then how canst thou contend with horses? and if in the land of peace, wherein thou trustedst, they wearied thee, then how wilt thou do in the swelling of Jordan?"* (Jeremiah 12:5).

God had not called him to run with the footmen. He had not called him to compare his lot with the lot of the wicked. If Jeremiah was willing to reduce himself to that level, how was he going to be ready for the greater challenges that lay ahead? How was he going to "contend with horses"?

As time runs out on the evil one, he will fight more desperately. He will pull out his best weapons and unleash his best soldiers. It is for that time that we prepare, refusing to be wearied by the low-level battles of daily living so that we can cross over.

It will not be enough in the last days to lead with the minimum amount of faith that it takes to get by. We cannot afford to have just enough faith to make the journey from Egypt to Pi-hahiroth by the sea (Exodus 14:9). Such faith will not enable us to go through the obstacles the enemy will place in our way. God's promises to us are not at Pi-hahiroth, but beyond. We cannot get to them without breakthrough faith.

What is breakthrough faith? It is the faith that enables us to deal with worst-case scenarios. It is the level of faith that makes it possible for us to go through the biggest obstacles we will encounter.

The apostle Paul did everything in his power to have that kind of faith. He could not be wearied by envy because according to Philippians 4:12, he had learnt

> *"both how to be abased and I know how to abound: every where and in all things I am instructed both to be full and to be hungry, both to abound and to suffer need."*

He sought to prepare himself to deal with the worst-case scenarios not by being preoccupied with the inequities around him, but by seeking to know Christ and the power of His resurrection (Philippians 3:10). He understood that it was only through that power that raised Christ from the dead that he could contend with horses and go through the "swelling of Jordan" ["the thickets of the Jordan"(NAB), "the thick thornbushes along the Jordan River" (NCV) and "the jungle of the Jordan" (RSV)].

Paul raised the bar for himself, training above everyone else's level, and refusing to exercise his leadership at the level of the ordinary. In the previous chapter, we saw how Daniel and his friends also raised the bar for themselves. As a result, when the challenges came, they were more than ready for them. Warned in Daniel 3 that if they did not bow to Nebuchadnezzar's golden statue, they would be thrown into the fiery furnace, the Hebrew boys responded (Daniel 3:17-18):

> *"If it be so, our God whom we serve is able to deliver us from the burning fiery furnace, and he will deliver us out of thine hand, O king.* **_But if not_***, be it known unto thee, O king, that we will not serve thy gods, nor worship the golden image which thou hast set up."* (emphasis added).

Notice how high they raised the bar. While they were confident that

God could rescue them from the judgment of King Nebuchadnezzar, it would not make a difference to their faith if He did not. Unlike the Jeremiah of Jeremiah 12:1-2 whose bellyaching suggested that the cause of the kingdom was not worth being poor for, the Hebrew boys were convinced it was worth dying for!

Their faith in God was not based on what God did or did not do for them. When our attitude towards God is not determined by what He does for us, we take away from the enemy one of his most potent weapons. When we know that the goodness of God is not defined by whether or not He answers our prayer for a brand new car, we make it impossible for Satan to use our lack to draw us away from God.

If God's goodness was determined by the fate of His children, then we would be justified on account of John's beheading, Jesus' death on the cross, the beatings endured by His disciples, the holocaust, the Rwandan genocide, to mention a few examples, to conclude that He is *not* a good God. Each negative thing that has happened to humanity over the ages would diminish His goodness and dim the brightness of His glory, leaving us with something undeserving of His name, an imperfect God not worth following, certainly not worth serving, and absolutely not worth dying for.

What the Hebrew boys were saying was that God does not change with a change in our fortunes. He does not become a better God because of our testimonies, the planes that we own or the great mansions in which we live. He does not become less good because we have lost a loved one or things are not going according to plan. He is good in spite of it all.

We tend to see a distorted image of God through the prism of our tragic experiences. Yet God is not what we see, but who He is. Asked by Moses who he would say had sent him to deliver the children of

Israel, God answered:

> *"I AM THAT I AM: and he said, Thus shalt thou say unto the*
> *children of Israel, I AM hath sent me unto you. And God said*
> *moreover unto Moses, Thus shalt thou say unto the children of*
> *Israel, The LORD God of your fathers, the God of Abraham,*
> *the God of Isaac, and the God of Jacob, hath sent me unto*
> *you: this is my name for ever, and this is my memorial unto all*
> *generations."* (Exodus 3:14-15).

We raise the bar when we recognize that I Am is His name forever. I Am is who He is. God is. He does not become what our experience wants Him to become. He is. Hebrews 11:6(b) tells us:

> *"...he that cometh to God must believe that **He is**, and is a*
> *rewarder of those who diligently seek Him".* (Emphasis added).

Before we get to the reward part, we must first of all know that He is. That must be settled in our doctrine. We must not let the reward part confuse us. What the Hebrew boys understood was that if they met their end in the fiery furnace, their reward in heaven was still secure. The reward is what we get when we go through the thickets of the Jordan in our diligent search for God. . While the "rewards" that we get during the journey might encourage us to persevere, the rewards that really count are those that come at the end.

When we know that, then we will not allow any negative experience between here and glory to diminish our zeal or to draw us away from God. In Job 1, Satan was convinced that Job's faith was based on the material things God had given him:

> *"Doth Job fear God for nought? Hast not thou made an hedge*
> *about him, and about his house, and about all that he hath*

on every side? thou hast blessed the work of his hands, and his substance is increased in the land. But put forth thine hand now, and touch all that he hath, and he will curse thee to thy face" (Job 1:9-11).

When God took everything away from Job, He fully expected him to remain standing. Job was not moved because he understood that God was not defined by the things He did for him. Confronted by his wife in Job 2:9 *("Dost thou still retain thine integrity? curse God, and die"),* Job took a leadership stand and refused to sin with his lips (Job 2:10).

Yet God was still angry with Job, making his displeasure plain in four chapters(38-41). How could God be angry with a man who had gone through so much, and who had even rejected his wife's counsel to curse Him? The fact is God did not just expect Job to pass this test. He expected him to pass it with flying colors. It is easy to slip when we dwell too long in a world of human wisdom. Notice that the exchanges between Job and his friends cover 33 chapters of the book of Job (4-37). God was not happy with Job for not recognizing that the enemy gnaws away at the faith of many through a war of attrition in which the words of human wisdom are his favorite weapons.

We also learn from the story of Job that God expects a leader's definition of crisis to be different from that of those he leads. Job's wife could get away with her foolishness because she was not the head of the house, but Job had to stand even for his wife's sake. In the end, she enjoyed the second wave of God's blessings with him because he took a stand (Job 42:10-17).

The children of Israel experienced the miracle of the parting of the Red Sea because Moses did not panic. Finding themselves hemmed in by the sea on the one side and the pursuing Egyptians on the other, the children of Israel cried out to the Lord in terror, and told Moses:

> *"Because there were no graves in Egypt, hast thou taken us away to die in the wilderness? wherefore hast thou dealt thus with us, to carry us forth out of Egypt? Is not this the word that we did tell thee in Egypt, saying, Let us alone, that we may serve the Egyptians? For it had been better for us to serve the Egyptians, than that we should die in the wilderness"* (Exodus 14:11-12).

Moses knew that it was through no error of judgment on his part that Israel was in that situation. It was God who had sent them that way (Exodus 14:1-2). If anyone was on the spot, it was God. If He had sent them into that trap, then He had already provided a way of escape, even though things certainly did not look that way.

Moses turned to the people and addressed them boldly:

> *"And Moses said unto the people, Fear ye not, stand still, and see the salvation of the LORD, which he will shew to you to day: for the Egyptians whom ye have seen to day, ye shall see them again no more for ever. The LORD shall fight for you, and ye shall hold your peace."* (Exodus 14:13-14).

This was not a moment of crisis. It was an opportunity for the Lord's glory to be revealed. When leaders approach the challenges that they encounter from that perspective, God responds to their faith in great ways. God expects us today to remember the example of Moses, and the words of I Corinthians 10:13, that *"…God is faithful, who will not suffer you to be tempted above that ye are able; but will with the temptation also make a way to escape…."*

We cannot abdicate the responsibility of leadership as a result of the hardships we encounter. We cannot lead by the lower standards that might guarantee our comfort but compromise our ability to accomplish His will. Leadership is not taking the path of least resistance, but traveling the high road in faith.

the CHALLENGE - ⟩ Can you run 🏔
with the best?

1. Why was Jeremiah's attitude in Jeremiah 12:1-2 dangerous?

2. What are your personal strategies for preparing for the worst-case scenarios?

3. What do you understand by the statement: God is not what you see, but who He is?

Personal lessons learned from Chapter 21

1.

2.

3.

"For by thee I have run through a troop; and by my God have I leaped over a wall."
- Psalm 18:29

TWENTY TWO

Raising the Bar II

"Let the dead bury their dead."

L U K E 9:60

*Only those who are willing
to wield the sword of truth
against themselves first
are fit for the kingdom.*

Jesus not only raised the bar, but was determined to raise leaders who did. The first order of business as He began His ministry was to put together a leadership team that could rise to the challenge of kingdom leadership.

He did not let the little detail that He was a largely untested leader deter Him from setting very high standards for His disciples. He certainly seemed to be assuring the failure of His recruitment drive by being so radical. What sensible person would be willing to meet these radical standards to follow the son of the neighborhood carpenter?

But then Jesus was not looking for "sensible" people. He was looking for those who were ready to hook in to a much greater purpose, people who could make radical personal choices for the cause.

When one of the men He had asked to follow Him requested permission to go and bury his father first, Jesus told him to get his priorities right:

> "...Let the dead bury their dead: but go thou and preach the kingdom of God" (Luke 9:60).

To another who wanted to go and bid farewell to those who were at his home before following the Lord, He said:

> "No man, having put his hand to the plough, and looking back, is fit for the kingdom of God" (Luke 9:61-62).

These requests were not unreasonable ones by normal standards. One would have expected Jesus to deal with them with more sensitivity. Was Jesus as coldhearted as these exchanges would seem to suggest?

As far as Jesus was concerned, there was a more important issue at stake here, and that was whether these men were ever going to be able to commit to pursuing God's purpose for their lives. He wanted them to understand that the enemy will use even seemingly reasonable things to lure people into emotional entrapments that void God's plans for their lives.

Would the man who wanted to go and bury his father be able to resist the pressure by the grieving family to take on more responsibilities in the family? The second man would most likely have had to explain to his family why he had decided to abandon everything to follow Jesus. What if the family was convinced that following Jesus was not the right thing to do? Would he have defied their collective wisdom to pursue God's purpose for his life?

Jesus raised the bar from the start because His purpose was to raise a leadership that was "fit for the kingdom". The last thing He needed was an emotionally fragile team that could not rise to the demands of kingdom leadership. He wanted it understood that it was one thing to be a leader, and quite another to be a kingdom leader.

The call to kingdom leadership was not a call to Amityville, according to Matthew 10:34-37:

> *"Think not that I am come to send peace on earth: I came not to send peace, but a sword. For I am come to set a man at variance against his father, and the daughter against her mother, and the daughter in law against her mother in law. And a man's foes shall be they of his own household. He that loveth father or mother more than me is not worthy of me: and he that loveth son or daughter more than me is not worthy of me."*

To pass the entrance exam into kingdom leadership, aspiring leaders had to learn to turn the sword of truth on themselves to sever all emotional strings that could compromise God's purpose for their lives. They had to win some very personal battles. Since it is often through our personal circumstances that the enemy diminishes our ability to respond to the demands of leadership, it is imperative that we also win our personal battles.

Not everyone is blessed with the circumstances into which John the Baptist was born. Not everyone has parents who are willing to fight their battles so that God's plan for their lives can be fulfilled. For many years, Zechariah the priest and his wife Elisabeth had been childless. One day, an angel of the Lord appeared to Zechariah and said:

> *"Fear not, Zacharias: for thy prayer is heard; and thy wife*

Elisabeth shall bear thee a son, and thou shalt call his name John" Luke 1:13.

In addition to specifically giving Zechariah the name they were to call the child (*"thou shalt call his name John"*), the angel announced that God had very important plans for John's life:

> *"...he shall be great in the sight of the Lord, and shall drink neither wine nor strong drink; and he shall be filled with the Holy Ghost, even from his mother's womb. [16] And many of the children of Israel shall he turn to the Lord their God. [17] And he shall go before him in the spirit and power of Elias, to turn the hearts of the fathers to the children, and the disobedient to the wisdom of the just; to make ready a people prepared for the Lord"* (Luke 1:15-17).

After the child was born, the family's neighbors and relatives came for his circumcision, and promptly named him Zechariah after the father. When Elisabeth rejected the name, telling them he was to be named John, the family protested:

> *"...There is none of thy kindred that is called by this name"* (Luke 1:61).

As kingdom leaders, Zechariah and Elisabeth knew that the name and God's plan for their child were inseparable, and that they had to win the war with their relatives in order for God's plan not to be voided. To name John anything else other than what God had ordained would have been to reject God's plan for their son.

Because we cannot relate to the cultural context in which such stories took place, it is easy to fail to understand how much of a big deal this was. Yet from God's perspective and as we see from the story, Zechariah and Elisabeth's victory was very significant: Once Zechariah, who had been dumb throughout Elizabeth's pregnancy, had confirmed that the child was to be named John according to the angel's instructions, his tongue was miraculously loosed, and he began to speak. Witnessing the power of God's enabling which comes when we win our personal battles,

> *"...fear came on all that dwelt round about them: and all these sayings were noised abroad throughout all the hill country of Judaea. And all they that heard them laid them up in their hearts, saying, What manner of child shall this be!"* (Luke 1: 65-66).

Zechariah and Elisabeth were willing to do what had never been done before even if it was unpopular with those they loved. They would not allow family tradition to compromise their child's destiny.

Matthew 16:24 tells how personal the battle must become:

> *"Then said Jesus unto his disciples, If any man will come after me, let him deny himself, and take up his cross, and follow me."*

We must liberate ourselves not just from the emotional entanglements of family, but from ourselves. Jesus was not interested in what the men that He called brought. What He was interested in was what He could turn them into. They were to dump their egos, traditions, and all their emotional baggage and humanistic thinking at the door, and in their place, carry a personal and public reminder of their commitment to fulfill God's will for their lives.

Jesus made it clear that there was no room for any gray areas, or half-hearted commitments. The disciples were either with the program or they weren't. He expected them to make a very personal and very public commitment to the cause and to His leadership:

> *"He that is not with me is against me: and he that gathereth not with me scattereth."* (Luke 11:23).

He certainly did not make it easy for anyone to be on His team. Many who tried simply could not make the cut. We read in John 6 that offended by His radical message, *"many of his disciples went back, and walked no more with Him."* (John 6:66.)

Not everyone left. When Jesus turned to the twelve and asked if they too were going to leave, Peter answered:

> *"Lord, to whom shall we go? thou hast the words of eternal life. And we believe and are sure that thou art that Christ, the Son of the living God"* (John 6:68-69).

To whom would they go? They had burned every bridge, leaving them with no way of retreat. More than that, all of them (with the exception of Judas Iscariot) had truly connected, and made a life commitment to the cause.

Jesus raised the bar because the issues at stake were too important. There was a sense of urgency about it all. He was soon going to be betrayed and crucified, and thereafter leave to be with the Father in heaven. By then, the disciples had to be ready to be about the business of the Father. He had to leave the work of the kingdom in the right hands.

Jesus raised the bar so that when the disciples were in the battlefield, they would not be fatally distracted. It was largely because they rose to the challenge of a higher standard of leadership that they succeeded. We too shall succeed when we can make the tough choices that will be required of those who God calls to make a difference in our time.

the CHALLENGE - > Are you fit for
the kingdom?

1. How important is the ability to make tough personal choices to the practice of leadership?

2. What role does God expect our families to play in determining our destinies?

3. What do you understand by the statement: Jesus raised the bar so that when the disciples were in the battlefield, they would not be fatally distracted?

Personal lessons learned from Chapter 22

1.
2.
3.

"No man that warreth entangleth himself with the affairs of this life."
- 2 Timothy 2:4

TWENTY THREE

Raising the Bar III

"How is it that thou,
being a Jew,
askest drink of me,
which am a woman
of Samaria?."

J O H N   4:9

The Spirit of God empowers us
for ministry without
social boundaries.

The story of Jesus' encounter with the woman of Samaria in John 4 was tricky on many levels. He was a Jew. She was a Samaritan. He was a single man, alone. She was a woman of questionable morals, also alone. He had a need. She had the means to meet His need.

Not willing to be held back by what was socially acceptable or safe, He surprised her with His request:

"Jesus saith unto her, Give me to drink" (John 4:7).

Suspicious, the woman asked Him in return:

*"How is it that thou, being a Jew, askest drink of me, which am
a woman of Samaria? for the Jews have no dealings with the
Samaritans"* (John 4:9).

The woman's reaction was perfectly understandable. The history of
animosity between the Jews and the Samaritans had been a long one.
The Jews largely considered the Samaritans unclean, and would often
bypass Samaria as they traveled between Judea and Galilee. In Luke
9 the Samaritans would not even allow Jesus to pass through their
village on His way to Jerusalem:

*"And it came to pass, when the time was come that he should be
received up, he stedfastly set his face to go to Jerusalem, [52] And
sent messengers before his face: and they went, and entered into
a village of the Samaritans, to make ready for him. [53] And they
did not receive him, because his face was as though he would go
to Jerusalem."*

The Samaritans considered it the ultimate insult that Jesus wanted
to pass through their village on His way to Jerusalem, the venerated
place of worship for the Jews, when they believed Mount Gerizim
was the mountain of God where everyone was supposed to worship.

Angered by the Samaritans' prejudice, Jesus' disciples (James and
John) asked Him for permission to call down fire from heaven to
burn them up as Elijah had done to the prophets of Baal (verse 54).
Jesus responded by rebuking them, saying:

*"Ye know not what manner of spirit ye are of. For the Son of
man is not come to destroy men's lives, but to save them."* Luke
9:55-56.

Jesus knew that He had a greater kingdom responsibility than to be offended by the response of the villagers from Samaria. He similarly would not let the Samaritan woman's response rob Him of an opportunity to minister to her. Discerning her spiritual need, He set aside His own to focus on hers:

> *"Jesus answered and said unto her, If thou knewest the gift of God, and who it is that saith to thee, Give me to drink; thou wouldest have asked of him, and he would have given thee living water"* (John 4: 10).

After explaining to her what He had to offer, she quickly forgot that she was dealing with a Jew and asked:

> *"Sir, give me this water, that I thirst not, neither come hither to draw"* (John 4:15).

By the end of His conversation with her, He had not only broken down the wall of separation, but had also won her soul, convincing her that He was the Messiah. Excited and renewed, she left her waterpot and ran into the city to invite everyone to meet the Lord. Many of the people of that city believed on account of what the woman told them, and even many more believed when they came to hear Him (verse 42).

In this story, the love of God for lost souls won over prejudice. Jesus would not withhold the gift of God on account of the woman's hostility, ethnicity or morality. He would not withhold it even though many of His own people thought the Samaritans were undeserving.

Kingdom leadership operates above social opinion. Jesus raised the bar by modeling that kind of leadership to His disciples. After His resurrection, He made it known that the Spirit of God would lead them to preach not just to the Jews, but also to those who were different from them:

> *"But ye shall receive power, after that the Holy Ghost is come upon you: and ye shall be witnesses unto me both in Jerusalem, and in all Judaea, and in Samaria, and unto the uttermost part of the earth"* (Acts 1:8).

The Spirit of God empowers us for ministry without social boundaries. His purpose is not for us to limit ourselves to the needs of our kind, but to win the lost irrespective of who they are.

We quench the Spirit when we attempt to contain Him in the boxes defined by our prejudices. The truth is that God created all of us in His image, and that He loves **all** of us equally, and that we **all** sinned and fell short of the Glory of God, and that He in response gave His only begotten Son do die for us **all**. The message of Romans 10:9-13 is for all:

> *"That if thou shalt confess with thy mouth the Lord Jesus, and shalt believe in thine heart that God hath raised him from the dead, thou shalt be saved. For with the heart man believeth unto righteousness; and with the mouth confession is made unto salvation. For the scripture saith, Whosoever believeth on him shall not be ashamed. For there is no difference between the Jew and the Greek: for the same Lord over all is rich unto all that call upon him. For whosoever shall call upon the name of the Lord shall be saved."*

The practice of the faith often comes loaded with the baggage of social history and tradition. It is God's desire that we see through His eyes. It is not good enough to say we cannot afford to be prejudiced because Jesus is coming soon. The implication would be that we simply don't want to be caught, but that if it were up to us, we would continue in the sin of prejudice. What God is looking for are hearts that can be changed by the truth of His word and the power of His grace.

There are many challenges that the issue of prejudice presents. It is an issue likely to offend someone irrespective of how it is dealt with. It is important to understand that God will judge prejudice just as much as He will judge the unforgiveness of those who have been victimized by it.

It is only love for truth that can change hearts. It is the love of truth that can save us from ourselves and from the evil one (2 Thessalonians 2:10). In the previous chapter, we saw how Peter responded when Jesus asked if the twelve were also going to leave Him like the others who had been offended by His words. Peter answered that they would not leave Him because He had "the words of eternal life" (John 6:68).

The challenge of kingdom leadership is how to bring those we lead to the depth of love for truth to which Jesus had brought the twelve. In John 8:31-32, Jesus suggests that we only come to knowledge of the truth and to the freedom it brings through continuing in the word. We can only love truth if we understand that the purpose of truth is to nourish, and not to offend. We must, through teaching, change the attitudes of those we lead towards the truth of God's word. There can be no freedom from prejudice without a change in our attitudes towards the word of truth.

When we love truth, we won't be able to ignore the fact that Miriam and Aaron's prejudice in Numbers 12:1-2 displeased God. We read in the Scriptures that they

> *"...spake against Moses because of the Ethiopian woman whom he had married: for he had married an Ethiopian woman.* [2] *And they said, Hath the LORD indeed spoken only by Moses? hath he not spoken also by us? And the LORD heard it."*

The Lord not only heard it, but also did something about it. His anger was kindled against Miriam and Aaron (verse 9), and as a result, *"Miriam became leprous, white as snow"*. Notice that the consequences of Miriam and Aaron's prejudice affected everyone. Because she was leprous and had to be shut out from the camp seven days, *"...the people journeyed not till Miriam was brought in again"* (verse 15). Israel came to a standstill.

The sin of prejudice is not the only one that can immobilize us. There are many other things that offend God greatly that we traditionally do not deal with. In Malachi 3:5, the Lord promises that He will be "a swift witness" not only against the sorcerers, adulterers, false swearers, but also against *"those that oppress the hireling in his wages... and that turn aside the stranger from his right...."*

James 5:4 puts it this way:

> *"Behold, the hire of the labourers who have reaped down your fields, which is of you kept back by fraud, crieth: and the cries of them which have reaped are entered into the ears of the Lord of sabaoth."*

The Lord is equally displeased with those "that turn aside the stranger from his right". The New Century Version puts it even clearer: "those who are unfair to foreigners". We cannot justify any unfairness towards a "stranger" or "foreigner" on the grounds that they are foreigners. We cannot exploit them on the grounds that they are ignorant of what is fair, or because they are desperate.

Kingdom leaders must make a commitment to fairness in their business practices, resisting the temptation to profiteer in the name of God. The voice of those who fear God and love the truth of His word must replace the voice of liberal humanists in matters of fairness and equity. We must reclaim the "moral" high ground others have occupied not because they have better values, but because we have defaulted.

It is time to take our place.

the CHALLENGE -

> **Placing equal value on God's people**

1. How valid is the statement that there can be no freedom from prejudice without a change in our attitude towards the truth of God's word?

2. In your opinion, should the standards of fairness that Christians adhere to be defined by such statutes as the law that prescribes a minimum wage for laborers?

3. Which is the greater sin, prejudice or the lack of forgiveness of those who are victimized by it?

Personal lessons learned from Chapter 23

| 1. |
| 2. |
| 3. |

"Of a truth I perceive that God is no respecter of persons."
- Acrs 10:34

TWENTY FOUR

Servant Leadership

And whosoever will be chief among you,
let him be your servant.

MATTHEW 20:27

Servant leaders
are those who can express
the nature of Christ the Lamb,
full of truth,
and Christ the Lion,
full of grace.

Much has been written lately about the importance of servant leadership. For a balanced view on the subject, we must defer neither to the traditions of our time nor the sensitivities of the age, but seek guidance from God's word and learn from the perfect example provided for us in Christ. When Christ and His word are the source of our guidance, we will escape the humanistic traps that make those who are decisive and confident in their leadership feel guilty for exercising authority, and those who serve with compassion feel weak.

The idea of servant leadership clearly has its basis in Scripture. The Word of God could not be clearer about the need for leaders to lead by serving.   In the words of Jesus in Matthew 20: 27-28:

> *"And whosoever will be chief among you, let him be your*
> *servant: even as the Son of Man came not to be ministered unto,*
> *but to minister, and to give His life a ransom for many".*

The word "chief" in this context means first in rank, influence or honor, or in other words, a leader.   What Jesus was saying was that whosoever would be a leader would need to be a servant.

What exactly did Jesus mean by a servant? In popular usage, a servant is one who is devoted to another to the disregard of his/her own interest, or one who gives himself/herself over to another person's will.   Jesus suggests His own leadership as an example of servant leadership, admonishing His disciples to be servants of that kind.

But what kind of servant was He?

Jesus served the people, ministered to them and put their interests first before His own.   It is also clear, however, that He never gave Himself over to their will.

According to John 2:23-25, when He was in Jerusalem at the Passover during the day of the feast, many were converted and believed in His name as a result of the miracles that He did.   He, however,

> *"...did not commit Himself unto them, because He knew all*
> *men, And needed not that any should testify of man: for He*
> *knew what was in man."*

Jesus understood that it was never God's intent to sentence leadership to the prison of the people's will.   He was sensitive to their needs, responding to them when it was in His power to do so as long as their demands did not divert Him from His call.

To Jesus, servant leadership meant not only leadership by serving but also serving by leading. The latter is a recognition that the leadership we provide is our service to God's people, even if it involves exercising the kind of authority people do not associate with a servant. While we may not naturally think of someone who exercises authority over us as a servant, Jesus calls His own resolute and decisive leadership servant leadership. He was being a servant, i.e. providing service in the interest of the people, by exercising the authority of a leader.

Clearly, we cannot overemphasize one aspect of servant-leadership over another without tragic consequences. When we overemphasize serving by leading, the result is authoritarian and self-serving leadership that does great harm to the cause of Christ. When we overextend the argument for leadership by serving, the result is leadership that is too overwhelmed by humanistic concerns to be effective in advancing God's purposes.

True servant leaders may not look like servants of the people at all according to our humanistic definition. The apostles were servant leaders who according to 2 Thessalonians 3:14 expected to be obeyed:

> *"And if any man obey not our word by this epistle, note that man, and have no company with him, that he may be ashamed."*

According to Paul, Titus' servant leadership was to be firm and decisive, and he was to *"speak, and exhort, and rebuke with all authority"*, allowing no man to despise his leadership (Titus 2:15). He was to remind the people to *"be subject to principalities and powers, to obey magistrates, to be ready to every good work"* (Titus 3:1).

Moses led by commandment. Joshua looked more like a general than a servant. It is important to understand that servant leaders are servants to God first, and that they serve man by being submitted to the will of God. They are servants to man by being submitted to God. They serve man by leading according to God's instructions.

The apostles understood that their servant-hood was not determined by doing whatever the people called on them to do. Their responsibility was to obey God as they served man. They were not any less humble in their service as leaders simply because their responsibility was not to wash the people's feet everyday or serve their tables.

In Acts 6, after a dispute arose between the Greek and Hebrew believers over some unfairness in food distribution, the twelve disciples told the people:

> *"It is not reason that we should leave the word of God, and serve tables"* (verse 2).

Some would consider such a statement arrogant and prideful, yet all it demonstrated was that the disciples knew their calling. They instructed the people to look for seven men to appoint over the business of food distribution so that they could remain focused on their mission:

> *"But we will give ourselves continually to prayer, and to the ministry of the word"* (verse 4).

The needs of the Grecian widows were very real. The disciples could have dropped everything to attend to the distribution of food themselves to prove just how diligent they were as servants. An unbalanced approach to servant leadership would have seen the apostles becoming deacons and accomplishing more fairness in the distribution of food but neglecting their call. There would not have been an increase in the Word and no great multiplication of the disciples in Jerusalem as a result.

The definition of servant leadership must take into account Hebrews 13:17:

> *"Obey them that have the rule over you, and submit yourselves: for they watch for your souls, as they that must give account, that they may do it with joy, and not with grief: for that is unprofitable for you."*

God expects the people to obey servant leaders. According to 2 Kings 18:11-12, the king of Assyria carried Israel into captivity in Assyria because *"they obeyed not the voice of the LORD their God, but transgressed his covenant, and all that Moses the servant of the LORD commanded, and would not hear them, nor do them."* When we do not obey those who serve us in leadership, we rob ourselves of God's blessings and His protection.

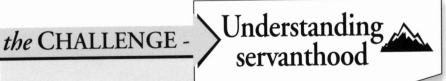

the CHALLENGE - > Understanding servanthood

1. How did biblical leaders deal with the challenge of providing firm and decisive leadership while remaining servants to those they led?

2. Was the centurion in Matthew 8 a servant-leader?

3. What kind of leadership did Jesus model for His disciples?

Personal lessons learned from Chapter 24

1.
2.
3.

"True servant leaders may not look like servants of the people at all according to our humanistic definitions."
- Author

TWENTY FIVE

Finishing

I have fought a good fight,
I have finished my course,
I have kept the faith:
Henceforth there is laid up for me
a crown of righteousness,
which the Lord, the righteous judge,
shall give me at that day:
and not to me only,
but unto all them also
that love his appearing.

2 TIMOTHY 4:7-8

A frontliner is a finisher,
not a purposeless dribbler.

I could hear Magaya's bare feet steadily pounding the track behind me. Halfway through the race, any excitement I had felt at the start had all but evaporated as it dawned on me that there was a world of difference between the 400-meter race and the 200 and 100-meter dashes at which I excelled.

I had entered the race for one reason only: to beat Magaya, an accomplished and gangly long distance runner my high school friends and I loved to foil. When the starter pistol went off, I was first out of the blocs and pulled away as Magaya maintained a steady and disciplined pace a few feet behind, waiting for my inevitable expiration just beyond the 200 meter mark.

I knew that getting to the 300-meter mark was not beating Magaya. I was running according to 1 Corinthians 9:24, to win, not to be among the many "also rans":

> *"Know ye not that they which run in a race run all, but one receiveth the prize? So run, that ye may obtain."*

As we rounded the bend for the final stretch, I could not believe how far the finishing line was. My desperate panting contrasted sharply with Magaya's rhythmic grunt as he steadily picked up speed. I clawed at the air and willed myself forward, knowing that losing the race would be disastrous for my reputation among my friends. A few yards from the tape I somehow surged forward, managing to cross the finish line barely two yards ahead of Magaya before passing out.

Thankfully I expired beyond the line. Beating Magaya more than made up for the indignity of passing out. The fact that in the final stretch I was taking three frantic steps for every one he took, that my chest felt like it was on fire, and I was seeing stars and hearing voices mocking my strength, did not in any way diminish my accomplishment.

It is not good enough for us just to respond to the call. We must finish what we begin. Jesus did not see His assignment simply in terms of doing, but finishing:

> *"...My meat is to do the will of him that sent me, and to finish*

his work." John 4:34.

In John 5:36 He told His disciples that the Father gave Him work *"to finish"*, and in Luke 9:62:

> *"...No man, having put his hand to the plough, and looking back, is fit for the kingdom of God".*

The message from Jesus was clear: God is looking for people who are committed to finishing. Those who look back are likely to abandon their kingdom assignments, making them unfit for the kingdom.

The apostle Paul was committed to finishing. In Acts 20:24 he wrote about not allowing adversity to stop him from finishing his assignment:

> *"But none of these things move me, neither count I my life dear unto myself, so that I might finish my course with joy, and the ministry, which I have received of the Lord Jesus, to testify the gospel of the grace of God."*

We will encounter much along the journey to dampen our enthusiasm. What will carry us to the finishing line is not mere enthusiasm. The journey of leadership is too long to be dependent on adrenalin levels. God does not expect us to be merely pumped up for the moment, but committed for the long haul. While zeal may enable us to do exploits at a given time, it is faith and our knowledge of God's will that enables us to finish.

We cannot finish with leaking spiritual tanks. The Scriptures tell us about a last days generation that cannot contain the things of God, a generation that is *"ever learning, and never able to come to the knowledge of the truth"* (2 Timothy 3:7). While we may be conscientious in going to the "gas station" every Sunday morning to fill up, we will not be able to purposefully direct what we cannot contain towards accomplishing kingdom goals.

The integrity of a frontliner's spiritual tank must be unassailable. In Acts 6:8 we read that *"Stephen, full of faith and power, did great wonders and miracles among the people."* It was the fullness of his tank that enabled him to do great wonders and miracles among the people and which took him across the finish line:

> *"When they heard these things, they were cut to the heart, and they gnashed on him with their teeth. But he, being <u>full</u> of the Holy Ghost, looked up stedfastly into heaven, and saw the glory of God, and Jesus standing on the right hand of God, And said, Behold, I see the heavens opened, and the Son of man standing on the right hand of God. Then they cried out with a loud voice, and stopped their ears, and ran upon him with one accord, And cast him out of the city, and stoned him: and the witnesses laid down their clothes at a young man's feet, whose name was Saul. And they stoned Stephen, calling upon God, and saying, Lord Jesus, receive my spirit"* (Acts 7:54-59).

The apostles were unstoppable in the book of Acts, charging ahead with the confidence of those who knew that their tanks were full. They were not running for honorable mention, but to finish and win the race. They understood that they could ill-afford to waste precious spiritual resources going on endless rabbit trails at a time of war. They focused on what God had called them to.

In the game of soccer, the purpose of being on the frontline is not to show off one's dribbling skills but to go past the defenders to place the ball in the net. A good frontliner is a finisher, not a pointless dribbler. God expects frontliners to purposefully advance the goals of the kingdom, to run *"not as uncertainly,"* and to fight *"not as one that beateth the air,"* (1 Corinthians 9:26).

A frontliner makes the efforts of those who passed him the ball worthwhile. Those who break their legs in the process of building up a play break their legs in vain if we choose not to finish. We put value to the efforts of those who laid their lives down for the cause of Christ when we are finishers. Jesus' ministry made the ministry of John worthwhile. According to Mark 6:14-29, John lost his head for the cause of righteousness. Jesus honored the ministry of John by finishing. He had a moral responsibility to finish. Had He not finished, John would have lost his head in vain.

Like Jesus, we will discover that the hardest part of our journey will be towards the finishing line. The battle will become fiercest in the last quarter. It was in the last quarter that He was betrayed. It was in the last quarter that He was abandoned by His disciples. When He could have used some emotional support, they were nowhere to be seen. Yet He still crossed the finishing line.

We cannot give up before crossing the finishing line. We cannot allow the enemy to win by default. Too many people in the kingdom give up because there is not enough encouragement from the sidelines. What we forget is that it is not the opinions of people about how we are fighting that will matter in the end, but the judgment of the *"the righteous judge"* who sits at the finish line holding *"a crown of righteousness"* which He will give to all those who finish the race and who *"love His appearing"* (2 Timothy 4:7-8).

the CHALLENGE - ▶ Finishing strong

1. What does it take to be able to stay the course of God's call for our lives?

2. Did Jesus finish His mission on earth or did Satan cut it short?

3. Are artistry and skill helpful or detrimental to the accomplishment of kingdom tasks?

Personal lessons learned from Chapter 25

1.	
2.	
3.	

"My meat is to do the will of Him that sent me, and to finish His work."
- John 4:34

TWENTY SIX

The Benefits Of The Call

Bless the Lord, O my soul:
and all that is within me,
bless His holy name.
Bless the Lord,
O my soul, and forget not
all His benefits.

PSALM 103:1-2

I will make of thee
a great nation,
and I will bless thee,
and make thy name great;
and thou shalt
be a blessing.

GENESIS 12:2

We have a difficult time accepting the call of God because we often think of it in terms of what we are asked to give up... (our jobs, our lifestyle, etc.) and we rarely focus on its clear benefits and the faithfulness of the One who does the calling.

Ultimately God's call is an invitation into His providence. He is clearly committed to those whom He calls. According to 2 Peter 1: 2-3 His servants have *"all things that pertain unto life and godliness"* by His divine power. We are not called to burdens, but rather *"to glory and virtue"*.

The Webster's New World College Dictionary defines glory as

1. Great honor and admiration won by doing something important or valuable; fame; renown;
2. The condition of highest achievement, splendor, prosperity etc.
3. Radiant beauty or splendor; magnificence etc.

We are called to great honor, praise, high achievement, prosperity, fame, and renown, among other things. If we understood this, surely we would be quick to respond to His call and to serve Him with great joy!

If we are called to glory and virtue, then clearly the call serves us more than it serves God. The devil has managed to convince many that they are called to make God look good at their expense. It is not possible to do anything to make God look any better. God cannot be improved upon. It is us who look better because of the call!

The blessings that come to those who obey the call are more than just rewards. As we see in Abraham's case, the blessings were part of the purpose of the call. Being made a great nation was part of the purpose of the call. Genesis 12:2:

> *"I will make of thee a great nation, and I will bless thee, and make thy name great; and thou shalt be a blessing".*

The miracle of Isaac was not a reward for obedience but rather the purpose of the call. The purpose of the call was for Sarah to be with child. The purpose of the call was to deal with her barrenness. How else could Abraham be the father of many nations except through him and his wife having a child? If we understood God's call to be a call to blessing, responding to it would not seem as much of a challenge.

Joseph was similarly called to be blessed. The blessings had to manifest in his life in order for him to fulfill God's prophetic intent. What was God's prophetic intent? It was to bring the children of Israel to Egypt according to the word of the Lord spoken to Abram in Genesis 15:13-14:

> *"And He said unto Abram, Know of a surety that thy seed shall be a stranger in a land that is not theirs, and shall serve them, and they shall afflict them four hundred years. And also that nation whom they shall serve, will I judge: and afterward shall they come out with great substance".*

To bring that to pass, Joseph necessarily had to be an important man, a man of means and influence in Egypt. Only a blessed and strategically positioned Joseph would have made it possible for Jacob and his children to come and live in Egypt to escape the famine in Canaan.

It was God's call to glory and virtue that placed Joseph on the throne of Egypt. It was God's call to blessing that made him a king in a strange land.

The call of Moses was automatically a call to greatness. When God calls us to an impossible task, it is automatically a call to greatness. He was called to an impossible undertaking whilst being assured of its success.

> *"Come now therefore, and I will send thee unto Pharaoh, that thou mayest bring forth My people the children of Israel out of Egypt"* (Exodus 3:10).

> *"And He said, Certainly I will be with thee.."* (Exodus 3:12).

Moses' failure would have made God, who had promised Abraham that the children of Israel would escape Egyptian bondage after four hundred years, a liar. Moses was guaranteed great success because God had purposed deliverance for the children of Israel before Moses was called. When he was called, it was to an undertaking where only one outcome was possible: success.

The very fact that God calls us to things we know we are unable to do is a commitment on His part to be present in the undertaking, and to anoint us for the task at hand. It is a call to glory.

Joshua's call was a call to glory. As God promised in Joshua 1:2-5, every place that the sole of his foot was to tread upon was to be his, and no man was going to be able to stand before him

> *"all the days of thy life: as I was with Moses, so will I be with thee: I will not fail thee nor forsake thee".*

He was not being called to fail. Success and greatness were foreordained. It was God's intent for Joshua and the children of Israel to possess the land of Canaan. He had purposed this even before Joshua was born.

Gideon, a man with some self-esteem issues, was called to glory and assured greatness (Judges 6:14):

"And the Lord looked upon him, and said, Go in this thy might, and thou shalt save Israel from the hand of the Midianites: have I not sent thee?"

"Thou shalt save Israel"...Note that the Lord did not say "perhaps you will be able to save Israel". According to God, success for this man who did not think much of himself was guaranteed, hence the definitive:

"Thou shalt save Israel".

He would succeed to save Israel and be assured of greatness because that was God's intent and because God's presence in the undertaking was assured:

"And the Lord said unto him, Surely I will be with thee, and thou shalt smite the Midianites as one man" (verse 16).

Noah's life was spared by the call. Not to respond to God's call would have meant certain death for Noah. The call was his salvation.

Noah's ark was as much for him as it was for the rest of the members of his family. It preserved him from the judgment of God just as much as it did for the others who were with him in the ark.

What God is calling us to do may prove to be our shelter from the judgment that is upon this world. We must willingly serve God knowing that He preserves us through the calls He places on our lives.

When we are called, our preservation becomes a kingdom issue. According to 1 Chronicles 16:20-22, once God called Israel, her preservation became a kingdom issue. As the children of Israel went from place to place and from nation to nation,

> *"from one kingdom to another people; He suffered no man to do them wrong: yea, He reproved kings for their sakes, saying, Touch not Mine anointed, and do My prophets no harm".*

For them to be harmed would have negated God's plan. God did not allow Israel to be harmed because anything that happened to them had kingdom implications.

Those who accept God's call end up dwelling *"in the secret place of the most High"* and abiding *"under the shadow of the Almighty"* (Psalm 91:1).

When we accept the call, we make the Lord our habitation and guarantee ourselves heavenly preservation. The promise of God's word is that neither evil nor plague shall befall us nor come near our dwelling, and that He will give His angels the responsibility to keep us in all our ways:

> *"They shall bear thee up in their hands, lest thou dash thy foot against a stone. Thou shalt tread upon the lion and adder: the young lion and the dragon shalt thou trample under feet."*
> (Psalm 91:12-13).

When the king of Syria was determined to silence Elisha, he sent an army complete with horses and chariots to apprehend him. When Elisha's servant saw the army, he was terrified. Elisha, aware of the supernatural hedge of protection God had put around him, told his servant not to be afraid:

"for they that be with us are more than they that be with them." (2 Kings 6:16).

Then Elisha prayed that the Lord would open the eyes of the young man. When the Lord opened his eyes, the servant saw that the mountain was *"full of horses and chariots of fire round about Elisha"* (2 Kings 6:15-17).

When we accept His call, we dwell in that place where all things work together for our good:

> *"And we know that all things work together for good to them that love God, to them who are the called according to His purpose"* (Romans 8:28).

The first three words of this Scripture are very important: "And we know." Paul knew that this was true for all those who were called according to God's purpose. He understood God's commitment and promises to those He had called. It was a living reality in his life and the lives of those with whom he served.

May it be a living reality in yours.

the CHALLENGE – 〉 Appreciating His Blessings

1. How are God's blessings not just a reward for obeying the call, but a part of the purpose of the call?

2. How does the call serve us more than it serves Him?

3. What do you understand by the statement that God's call is ultimately an invitation into His providence?

Personal lessons learned from Chapter 26

1.	
2.	
3.	

"(God) is a rewarder of them that diligently seek Him."
- Hebrews 11:6

EPILOGUE

At a Leadership conference organized by the head of a large Christian ministry, I observed the conference host furiously taking notes even when leaders of much smaller ministries were speaking.

The truth is that the greatest leaders don't stop learning until they cross the threshold to glory. They are just as willing to learn from others as much as they make themselves available to share their experiences. It is from this exchange that we are all raised to a higher level of faith and effectiveness as we seek to advance the kingdom.

I offer this book in the spirit of that exchange. Like many others who have written on the subject of leadership, I am under no illusion that you will get all the answers you need from this book. We come to completion by filling in the blanks from the input of different people to whom the Lord has committed various parts of the kingdom picture.

I am hopeful that what you have found in this work has spurred you to study the Scriptures which must be the ultimate source of completion in our leadership quest.

As important as this book may be, it cannot replace the real playbook that God has given you, which is His word in the form of the Bible.

I would encourage you to use the personal study guide at the end of each chapter and the group study guide that follows to begin a serious study of what the word of God says concerning leadership.

I believe we are at a critical time in God's calendar, and that He is looking to raise a cadre of leaders who are interested in discovering the fullness of His truth. The challenge to you is to consult the whole playbook, even if it affects your denominational game plan. Because it is time to begin the engraving process on the side of the coins of truth that we have left blank for so long, it is my belief that God will raise a generation of Kingdom leaders whose purpose is not to uphold tradition, but to bring completion.

God is looking for people who are not trying to create the Gospel. Our responsibility is not to make the bread of life, but to feed the Lord's sheep. Our responsibility is to give the people of God what has already been made in God's kitchen. If the only thing that this book has done is to bring you to the recognition that this is the kind of leadership the Lord is looking for, it will have accomplished half of its purpose.

In the opening chapter of this book, I talked about the river of God's purpose as a detour. On God's map, God's way is the way and ours the detour. On our own maps, His is the detour and ours the way. If this book has given you the confidence to shred your own map and adopt His, and to change your view to believe that God's way is in fact not the detour, but The Way, then this book will have accomplished the second half of its purpose.

I also want to encourage you to purchase this book for others. When you do, you are supporting our efforts to respond to the challenge of leadership. To know more about our work and to partner with us, feel free to contact us .

For bookings for our *"Frontline Leadership Seminars,"* speaking engagements, and/or to order more copies of *"The Challenge of Leadership"* or for more information on upcoming books, please contact our publisher.

Many blessings,
Noah N. Manyika

P.O. Box 32454
Charlotte NC 28232
U.S.A.

GROUP STUDY GUIDE

1
Scriptures for Group Study:

Exodus 3:1-12
Matthew 19:20-24
Judges 6:11-24
Proverbs 19:21
Acts 9:1-9

GROUP REFLECTION

When you see God's signposts on the road of your life, do you pay
attention to them? Are you able to see and willing to obey God's flashing
detour signs?

TOPICS FOR GROUP DISCUSSION:

Discuss the following challenges:

1. Distinguishing between God's redirection of our lives, and the
   enemy's disruption.
2. Obeying the call without all the details of the plan.
3. Walking purposefully in unfamiliar territory.
4. Staying the course of God's detour.

Conclude the study session with a time of prayer and declaration of
commitment by each participant to follow God's plan for their lives.

2
Scriptures for Group Study:

Luke 19:40
Isaiah 6:1-8
Galatians 1:15-17
1 Kings 19:19-21

GROUP REFLECTION

Isaiah's experience was an awesome one. He **saw** the Lord in His glory.
Like the angels who worship God day and night, the significance of
his experience was not lost on him. Once cleansed of His sin, he knew
there was only one thing to do: be available to serve this awesome God
everyday and night.

TOPICS FOR GROUP DISCUSSION:

Discuss the following challenges:

1. Responding to the call when you are not God's specific choice.
2. Positioning yourself to be sent.
3. Understanding what an experience with God is telling you about what you should be doing for the kingdom.
4. Making God know you are available.

Conclude the study session with a time of prayer and declaration of
commitment by each participant to be available to be sent by God.

Great leaders achieve success by allowing themselves to be interrupted by God, and by staying the course of God's detour.

God interrupts our lives to bring us into the stream of His power, and to line us up with His purpose.

Our path to destiny often begins with a collision with the rushing river of God's purpose. Human nature demands that we build a bridge over it, but the call of God directs us to step in and be swept away.

POINTS TO PONDER *for* 1 & 2

God does not call us out of lack on His part. If He needs us, it is because He chooses to need us.

Availability is a function of choice. God expects us to draw His attention to our availability.

Those who exit their experience with God without making the decisions called for by that experience will find it difficult to make the decisions afterwards.

3
Scriptures for Group Study:

> 1 Samuel 17:26-50
> Ezra 10:1-4
> Esther 4:1-16
> Numbers 25:6-13

GROUP REFLECTION

Decrying the indifference of those who refused to challenge the evil of segregation in South Africa, a civil rights activist remarked: "There are none so blind as those who wish not to see". Do you see what God wants you to see? Are your eyes open to the causes with which God wants you to connect?

TOPICS FOR GROUP DISCUSSION:

Discuss the following challenges:

1. Identifying your cause.
2. Responding to the call of the cause when God has not spoken directly to you.
3. Drawing faith from what God has done in the past and deploying that faith to address present challenges.
4. Escaping relationship traps that affect your ability to respond to your cause.

End the study session with a time of prayer and declaration of commitment by each participant to identify the cause with their name written on it, and to respond to its call.

4
Scriptures for Group Study:

Judges 4:1-9
Matthew 1:18-25
Luke 12:48(b)

GROUP REFLECTION

Jesus willingly left His throne in heaven to pay a debt He did not owe. He fulfilled the responsibility of sonship by going where God sent Him and accomplishing that for which He was sent. Can you fulfill the responsibility of sonship by responding to the call of kingdom duty?

TOPICS FOR GROUP DISCUSSION:

Discuss the following challenges:

1. Responding with a sense of duty to a situation you were not responsible for creating and from whose resolution you stand to gain nothing.
2. Releasing others with whom you are emotionally involved to respond to the call of kingdom duty.
3. Combining our sense of duty with the passion of believing to give a cutting edge to our response to the call of duty.
4. Attaching value to the things that are freely given.

Conclude the study session with a time of prayer and declaration of commitment by each participant to be willing to be drafted into kingdom duty and not to stand in the way of others.

To David, the taunts of the Philistine and his defiance of the armies of the living God were a call to leadership.

We must have the emotional strength to send unequivocal messages to colleagues, compatriots, relatives and friends that while we love them, we will not allow them to stand in the way of our destinies.

Goliath was challenging not just Israel but the kingdom of God itself. Because this was a kingdom issue, there was no way David could fail.

POINTS TO PONDER *for* 3 & 4

Those who do not know that they have been given much will exempt themselves from the requirement to respond to the call of duty.

When we run away from the responsibilities of sonship, we merely confirm to God that we don't believe we were ever enriched by the blessing of His grace.

When we combine a sense of duty with the passion of believing, we give our response to the call of the cause a cutting edge.

5
Scriptures for Group Study:

Hebrews 3:7-8
Judges 10:16
Luke 12:34
Luke 19:41-44
John 11:33-36

GROUP REFLECTION

God is looking for hearts that can be moved by the misery of Israel and the despair of Samaria, hearts that can be touched by the infirmities of others. How sensitive are you to the needs of others?

TOPICS FOR GROUP DISCUSSION:

Discuss the following challenges:

1. Weeping over the blindness of others.
2. Remaining emotionally engaged in the needs of those you leave behind as you ascend the social ladder.
3. Surrendering your cares to His providential care so your heart can be moved by the things that move His.
4. Balancing compassion with practicality.

Conclude the study session with a time of prayer and declaration of commitment by each participant not to harden their heart.

6
Scriptures for Group Study:

Psalm 16:5
Judges 6:16
Genesis 28:15
Exodus 33:15
Psalm 51:11
Isaiah 8:9-10

GROUP REFLECTION

God wants you to believe that He is enough. He wants you to believe that His presence in your call is more sufficient than all the provision you can create.

TOPICS FOR GROUP DISCUSSION:

Discuss the following challenges:

1. Responding to the call of God when you have limited material resources.
2. Understanding the relevance of God's presence to the practicalities of your call.
3. Planning on His miraculous provision for your journey.
4. Knowing the reality of His presence.

Conclude the study session with a time of prayer and declaration of commitment by each participant to trust in the Lord's sufficiency and value His presence in their lives.

We sink our roots so deep into the business of living that we are not easily moved even when the call of the cause is loud and clear.

By its very nature, Godly compassion is disruptive, forcing generosity of time and resources in violation of the carefulness of business.

We cannot free our hearts to be moved by the things that move God's heart without surrendering the business of living to His providential care.

POINTS TO PONDER *for* 5 & 6

The key to Israel's victories over her enemies was the Emmanuel Factor.

Our anxiety about resources betrays a lack of understanding that great exploits in the Scriptures are not a triumph of material resources, but of the presence of God in His purpose.

We must respond to the challenge of leadership not because of what we can do through the resources that we have, but because we discern God's prophetic intent and allow Him to fulfill it through us.

7
Scriptures for Group Study:

Galatians 1:16-19
Matthew 3:13-17
1 Kings 19:20-21

GROUP REFLECTION

The God-process of transition as presented in the Scriptures is often too messy for our generation's comfort. Yet the kingdom leaders who succeeded did so despite the "messy" transitions. What is important is not how impressive the transitional plan is, but whether or not God accomplishes in us what He intends during our transition.

TOPICS FOR GROUP DISCUSSION:

Discuss the following challenges:

1. Knowing what to do after the prophet has departed.

3. Identifying the right mentor.

4. Submitting to the God-process of transition that guarantees an open heaven.

Conclude the study session with a time of prayer and declaration of commitment by each participant to allow the hand of God to direct their transition to the next stage of their journey.

8
Scriptures for Group Study:

Psalm 121:3-8
Luke 9:1-6
Luke 10:1-17

GROUP REFLECTION

Not only do you have the preeminent instructor in God, you have the ultimate keeper, protector and upholder. He is an ever present help in the trouble of your learning experience, not only making sure that you don't fall off and hurt yourself, but also that you acquire the skills necessary to do the job.

TOPICS FOR GROUP DISCUSSION:

Discuss the following challenges:

1. Drawing confidence from God's confidence in us.

2. Dealing with the obstacles on the way.

3. Learning to trust your judgment.

Conclude the study session with a time of prayer and declaration of commitment by each participant to lean on God and not on their ability as they learn from the saddle.

The Lord will often leave us with nothing more to start with than the knowledge that He has called us.

Jesus knew better than to allow the skepticism of others to stop Him from walking in His calling.

Jesus understood that humility was not only the way to God's heart, but also the way up.

POINTS TO PONDER *for* 7 & 8

Those who are unwilling to endure the humiliation of learning never become the people God wants them to be.

God's leaders are made in motion. He sets us on the saddle to fashion us through the dynamic motion of the calls and the moulding of His hands.

Some of our mistakes and failures are so old that it takes an unbelievable amount of pride to think that anyone remembers them, or that it makes any difference if they do.

9
Scriptures for Group Study:

Hebrews 13:17
Colossians 1:16
Matthew 8:8-12

GROUP REFLECTION

As we fight to set the church free from harmful legalism and unproductive and stifling traditions, each one of us is responsible for the brick we remove and the contribution we make to lawlessness in the house of the Lord. In our zeal for liberty, we must remember to honor and leave untouched the structures of accountability that God established.

TOPICS FOR GROUP DISCUSSION:

Discuss the following challenges:

1. Submitting to authority when you are a leader.

2. Submitting to the authority of someone who has less material means than you.

3. Accepting inequality of rank and privilege as part of God's design.

Conclude the study session with a time of prayer and declaration of commitment by each participant to honor God's structures of accountability and to submit to Godly authority.

10
Scriptures for Group Study:

Romans 8:28
Psalm 139:8-10
Psalm 20:1
Psalm 27:5
Psalm 46:1
Luke 21:25-26
Proverbs 3:25

GROUP REFLECTION

When we respond appropriately to trouble, visions are birthed, movements are launched, heroes are made. See in trouble the opportunity to begin.

TOPICS FOR GROUP DISCUSSION:

Discuss the following challenges:

1. Discovering God's purpose for your life in your day of trouble.

2. Finding guidance from God's word to help you through trouble.

3. Encouraging yourself in the Lord in your day of trouble.

4. Dealing with sudden trouble in faith.

End the study session with a time of prayer and declaration of commitment by each participant to let their faith inform their response to the challenge of trouble.

The prophets of old were adept at dividing the issues, speaking the truth to kings even as they honored their offices.

In God's kingdom, inequality of rank is not inequality of worth.

Where God places us in His hierarchical formation and when He chooses to promote us is His sovereign prerogative.

POINTS TO PONDER *for* 9 & 10

Nothing imposes clarity of vision and compels efficiency of action quite like trouble.

We must see in our trouble the opportunity and the call to begin. When we allow trouble to victimize us, we become unable to take hold of our destiny.

We must not allow the devil to convince us that the Lord's outstretched hand of redemption is unreachable from the depth of the pits we dig ourselves.

11
Scriptures for Group Study:

1 Kings 18:21
2 Kings 6:11-23
2 Timothy 3:1-9
Romans 1:16-32

GROUP REFLECTION

When we forget that the battle is won on the frontlines, we virtually guarantee the enemy's victory.   When our only strategy is retreat, and we abandon the frontlines to withdraw into the safety of our churches, we make his job of taking over the courts, schools, hospitals, media, and even our homes a very easy one.

TOPICS FOR GROUP DISCUSSION:

Discuss the following challenges:

1. Having confidence in the invisible firewall of God's protection when you are in the line of fire.
2. Unsheathing the sword of truth in an age of political correctness.
3. Fighting passionately when the rest of the army does not see the need to fight.
4. Dealing with sudden trouble in faith.

Conclude the study session with a time of prayer and declaration of commitment by each participant to rise to the call of frontline leadership.

12
Scriptures for Group Study:

Psalm 82:5
1 John 2:15-16
Proverbs 29:2

GROUP REFLECTION

Can we see through the civilized covering of modernity to understand the true nature of the world in which we live? Are we closer to God because we are technologically advanced? What does God Himself think about our world?

TOPICS FOR GROUP DISCUSSION:

Discuss the following challenges:

1. Understanding liberal internationalism.
2. Understanding where the world is today on God's calendar.
3. Infusing a sense of historical purpose into the priorities of an a-historical generation to rally it to war against national and international liberalism.

Conclude the study session with a time of prayer for the Lord to open the eyes of all participants to see the true nature of the world in which they live.

We cannot afford to continue keeping the sharp edges of the Gospel hidden when the enemy has unsheathed his own weapons.

When we are on the frontline we are in the line of fire. What we must be able to discern are the invisible walls of God's protection.

Frontline leaders respond to the call of the cause even when those who will benefit do not appreciate it.

POINTS TO PONDER *for* 11 & 12

To provide definition to our leadership, we must know the nature of our world and where we are on God's calendar.

Frontliners cannot operate on assumptions about the world in which they live, but on truth.

We cannot afford to be so afraid of being swallowed up by the dragon the political process has become to concede the playing field to those who are committed to the complete dismantling of everything that is based on Christian values.

13
Scriptures for Group Study:

1 Corinthians 16:9
2 Samuel 4:1-7
2 Samuel 5:7
2 Samuel 5:10-12

GROUP REFLECTION

We often find ourselves in endless personal battles because we fail to discern the kingpins in our way. We can only discern the kingpins by the Spirit of God.

TOPICS FOR GROUP DISCUSSION:

Discuss the following challenges:

1. Identifying the Abners behind the shadows you have been fighting.
2. Understanding the importance of fasting and prayer in spiritual warfare.
3. Balancing zeal with knowledge.

Conclude the study session with a time of prayer for the Lord to bless all participants with a spirit of discernment.

14
Scriptures for Group Study:

John 5:19
Psalm 127:1
Proverbs 29:18
Habakkuk 2:2
Hebrews 11

GROUP REFLECTION

It is easy to stray from the script written in heaven for our lives. We have an example in the Christ of one who never strayed, and whose vision will continue accomplishing its purpose into eternity. It is an example worth emulating.

TOPICS FOR GROUP DISCUSSION:

Discuss the following challenges:

1. Translating God's will into a working vision.
2. Ensuring that your vision stays connected with its life source, which is the will of God.
3. Guarding against your initiative taking you away from the grace of God.

Conclude the study session with a time of prayer and declaration of commitment by each participant to maintain the life connection between their visions and God.

The promises of God are not easily possessed because it is the enemy's self-appointed job to interdict us.

We cannot count the battle to be won until the kingpin has fallen.

The young warriors of the faith tend to forget that wars are won through patient, informed determination, and that zeal without knowledge breeds a monochromatic spirituality that can discern neither the nuances of God's will nor the complexities of the battle.

POINTS TO PONDER *for* 13 & 14

Our investment in the development of vision must take into account the fact that not every cause requires a complicated response.

We must guard against becoming less and less dependent on God as we become more and more proficient at project planning and visioneering.

There are many big things that have been built without God "for God".

15
Scriptures for Group Study:

Hebrew 11:8
2 Corinthians 5:7
Hebrews 12:2

GROUP REFLECTION

Faith is the ingredient in our efforts that brings God joy. It is what makes our offering to Him acceptable. We cannot substitute it with human wisdom, or make up for its absence with education or enthusiasm.

TOPICS FOR GROUP DISCUSSION:

Discuss the following challenges:

1. Applying faith to the solving of every day "non-spiritual" problems.
2. Walking confidently in the progressive revelation of God's will.
3. Understanding the relationships between faith and the anointing.
4. Understanding the responsibility of the anointing.

Conclude the study session with a time of prayer for each participant to be strengthened in their faith.

16
Scriptures for Group Study:

Joshua 1:1-2
Psalm 37:23-24
John 14:12

GROUP REFLECTION

The great leaders who went before us were required by God to walk their own walk of obedience. They did, with His help. He expects us to walk our own, and we must, with His help.

TOPICS FOR GROUP DISCUSSION:

Discuss the following challenges:

1. Building on a successful foundation.
2. Dealing with people's expectations.
3. Understanding God's grace for you.

Conclude the study session with a time of prayer for each participant to draw confidence in their walk from what the Lord has done in them.

God expects us to walk confidently in the progressive revelation of His will.

The faith of the great leaders of biblical times was very relevant to the solving of practical problems and accomplishing of both "secular" and spiritual tasks.

Jesus is not interested in equipping us to take shortcuts to glory. He anoints our faith to enable us to accomplish God's purposes according to His will.

POINTS TO PONDER *for* 15 & 16

We put unbearable and unnecessary pressure on ourselves when we do not recognize that leadership shoes are cut to size.

God calls us to a personal expression of His purpose.

Ultimately, any leader is a tough act to follow if we operate under the misapprehension that we can succeed without relying on God.

17
Scriptures for Group Study:

Joshua 23:10
Phillipians 4:13
Deuteronomy 32:30
Exodus 18:18

GROUP REFLECTION

God is The Power of One through whom we can do all things. It is only through Him that we can excel for His kingdom against all odds.

TOPICS FOR GROUP DISCUSSION:

Discuss the following challenges:

1. Believing that His presence can make a difference when the odds are against us.
2. Applying the idea of the power of one to practical life situations.
3. Knowing when to ask for help.

Conclude the study session with a time of prayer and declaration of commitment by each participant that they will believe God, not the odds.

18
Scriptures for Group Study:

Luke 4:1
Daniel 4:29-37
Hebrews 11:36-38
Nehemiah 9:19-21
1 Chronicles 12:1

GROUP REFLECTION

When you have given your life wholly to God, He will lead you through the veldts and valleys, and through the wilderness, and through anything and anywhere to establish His purpose in you.

TOPICS FOR GROUP DISCUSSION:

Discuss the following challenges:

1. Reconciling being in the wilderness and being in God's will.
2. Feeling God's presence in the wilderness.
3. Surviving the tests of the wilderness experience.

End the study session with a time of prayer for all participants to develop the patience, fortitude and wisdom of David who remained in the wilderness until God's work was accomplished in Him.

Behind every dazzling and supernatural leadership success is the prophetic promise of God for that particular outcome and His direct involvement in the activity leading to it.

God's great force multipliers are people who walk in obedience and know and trust the God method.

An important part of leadership is knowing when to ask for help and when to stop hiding our need from those God has sent to help us.

POINTS TO PONDER *for* 17 & 18

The uncomfortable reality the Bible confronts us with is that the wilderness experience is as much for the obedient and humble as it is for the Nebuchadnezzars of this world.

The wilderness is a place where God's purpose in us is tested and strengthened.

When we retreat to our places of refuge, not out of fear of the enemy but out of obedience to God, He is just as pleased as when we are charging forward to conquer and vanquish in obedience to His command.

19
Scriptures for Group Study:

Luke 21:16-19   John 13:26-27
John 6:64-70   Matthew 26:42
Matthew 20:18-19
2 Timothy 3:1-4

GROUP REFLECTION

We must never allow our pain to rob us of the important lessons we must learn from the school of betrayal. Our preoccupation with our Judases must not rob us of our ability to respond to God's open invitation to move forward.

TOPICS FOR GROUP DISCUSSION:

Discuss the following challenges:

1. Accepting betrayal as an occupational hazard and a last days fact of life.
2. Finding God's purpose in very personal pain.
3. Forgiving the traitor and letting go of the hurt.
4. Forgiving those who fail to come to your defense when you are being betrayed.

Conclude the study session with a time of prayer and confession of the sin of unforgiveness. Allow the Spirit of God to minister to each participant in a personal way, and lead the participants in a time of commitment to let go of the hurt.

20
Scriptures for Group Study:

> 1 Samuel 13:13-14
> Acts 5:1-11
> Acts 16:9-10
> Daniel 1:8-16

GROUP REFLECTION

God expects you to walk your own personal walk, to follow the rules that He has set for you and to live by the manual inscribed with your name.

TOPICS FOR GROUP DISCUSSION:

Discuss the following challenges:

1. Understanding the unique demands of obedience God has placed on your life.
2. Dealing with the fact that others get away with things that God does not allow you to get away with.

Before concluding the session, read the article quoted in Chapter 20 again. End the session with a time of prayer for the participants to renew their commitment to obey God's commandments which are specific to them.

We must put Judas' treachery into perspective, recognizing that what seemed like a tragic episode in the ministry of Christ was not the end of the story.

We learn at Gethsemane that other people do not necessarily operate in the timing demanded by our emotional need.

Betrayal comes with the times and in spite of our good judgment.

POINTS TO PONDER *for* 19 & 20

God has a right to define the standards to which He will hold each individual He calls.

We stand logic on its head when we complain about God's expectation that we live up to the standards specific to our callings while demanding higher bracket rewards.

God is pleased when we set high standards of righteousness for ourselves.

21
Scriptures for Group Study:

Jeremiah 12:5
Philippians 4:12
Daniel 3:17-18
Hebrews 11:6
Job 1:9-11

GROUP REFLECTION

The call to kingdom leadership in the last days is not an ordinary call. The reason is because the last days are not ordinary days. We are living in times when the kingdom is under attack like never before. God wants to raise up the last day Joshuas, Calebs and Daniels who will respond to the challenge of leadership and roll-back the enemy's gains.

TOPICS FOR GROUP DISCUSSION:

Discuss the following challenges:

1. What will it take not to be distracted by envy in the last days?

2. How do you acquire breakthrough faith that enables you to deal with the worst-case scenarios and the challenges of the last days?

3. How do you raise the bar in prayer and fasting to be empowered by God for the last days?

Conclude the study session with a time of prayer and a commitment by each participant to increase their time for seeking the Lord in prayer and fasting.

22
Scriptures for Group Study:

> Luke 9:60-62
> Matthew 10:34-37
> Matthew 16:24
> Luke 11:23
> John 6:66-69

GROUP REFLECTION

Are you willing to fight the personal battles it takes to qualify for kingdom leadership?

TOPICS FOR GROUP DISCUSSION:

Discuss the following challenges:

1. Dealing with emotional traps.
2. Battling your family heritage.
3. Strategies for liberating you from yourself.
4. Understanding God's higher standards for kingdom leadership.

Conclude the study session with a time of prayer and a commitment by each participant to increase their time for seeking the Lord in prayer and fasting.

It will not be enough in the last days to lead with the minimum amount of faith that it takes to get by.

God expects a leader's definition of crisis to be different from that of those he leads.

We tend to see a distorted image of God through the prism of our tragic experiences. Yet God is not what we see, but who He is.

POINTS TO PONDER *for* 21 & 22

Jesus raised the bar because His purpose was to raise a leadership that was "fit for the kingdom," not an emotionally fragile team that could not rise to the demands of kingdom leadership.

Jesus made it clear that there was no room for any gray areas, or half-hearted commitments. The disciples were either with the program or they weren't.

Since it is often through our personal circumstances that the enemy diminishes our ability to respond to a higher calling, winning our personal battles will determine how far we can go in kingdom leadership.

23
Scriptures for Group Study:

John 4:6-42   Malachi 3:5
Luke 9:51-56   James 5:4
Numbers 12:1-2
John 8:31-32

GROUP REFLECTION

Because of the lateness of the hour, we cannot afford the fatal distractions that the issues of prejudice, unforgiveness and unfairness present. Can you make a commitment to be an agent of change in these areas?

TOPICS FOR GROUP DISCUSSION:

Discuss the following challenges:

1. The challenge of prejudice.
2. The challenge of unforgiveness.
3. Bringing ourselves and those we lead to the understanding that the purpose of truth is to nourish, not to offend; to liberate and not to condemn.
4. Understanding God's higher standards for kingdom leadership.

Conclude the study session with a time of prayer and declaration of commitment by each participant to address any of the areas discussed above that might be a challenge.

24
Scriptures for Group Study:

Matthew 20:27-28
Hebrews 13:17
Matthew 8:8-13
John 2:23-25
Acts 6:2
2 Kings 18:11-12

GROUP REFLECTION

Jesus was a servant-leader. He served by leading and led by serving. He found the critical balance necessary for effective leadership. He served boldly, but with compassion. He served with grace and truth.

TOPICS FOR GROUP DISCUSSION:

Discuss the following challenges:

1. Providing firm and decisive leadership while remaining servants to those you lead.
2. Protecting your call from the expectations of people (Acts 6:2).

Conclude the study session with a time of prayer and declaration of commitment by each participant to become the servant leaders that God expects them to be.

Kingdom leadership operates above social opinion.

We quench the Spirit when we attempt to contain Him in the boxes defined by our prejudices.

What God is looking for are hearts that can be changed by the truth of His word and the power of His grace.

POINTS TO PONDER *for* 23 & 24

Jesus understood that it was never God's intent to sentence leadership to the prison of the people's will.

The apostles were not any less humble in their service as leaders simply because their responsibility was not to wash the people's feet everyday or serve their tables.

To Jesus, servant leadership meant not only leadership by serving but also serving by leading.

25
Scriptures for Group Study:

2 Timothy 4:7-8
1 Corinthians 9:24-26
John 4:34
Luke 9:62
Acts 20:24

GROUP REFLECTION

Do you have what it takes to finish?   What is it that the giants of the faith had that enabled them to brush the enemy aside and press on towards the mark of God's calling? Do you have the patience to stay the course and to fight to the end?

TOPICS FOR GROUP DISCUSSION:

Discuss the following challenges:

1. Finding the grace to stay the course.
2. Running to win without crowd support.
3. Drawing strength from the value of the prize at the end of the race.

End the study session with a time of prayer and declaration of commitment by each participant to run the race to the end.

26
Scriptures for Group Study:

Genesis 12:2
Psalm 103
Genesis 15:13-14
Romans 8:28

GROUP REFLECTION

Being in God's will is always a winning proposition. Our victory will always swallow up any "triumphs" the enemy might seem to score on our journey. Nothing can be compared to the gift of eternal life which is our heritage. Yet God also blesses us in our earthly pilgrimage with blessings that far outweigh anything the enemy might bring against us. According to 2 Peter 1:1-3, He blesses us with "all things that pertain unto life and goldliness."

Conclude this final session with a prayerful reading of Psalm 103 by all participants as they rise to the challenge of leadership.

While zeal may enable us to do exploits at a given time, it is faith and our knowledge of God's will that enables us to finish.

The apostles were not running for honorable mention, but to finish and win the race.

In the game of soccer, the purpose of being on the frontline is not to show off our dribbling skills. The frontliner is a finisher, not a pointless dribbler.

POINTS TO PONDER *for* 25 & 26

The fact that God calls us to impossible tasks is a commitment on His part to be present in the undertaking and to anoint us for the task at hand.

We are not called to make God look good at our expense. It is not possible to do anything to make God look any better. God cannot be improved upon.

When we are called, our preservation becomes a kingdom issue. When we accept the call, we make the Lord our habitation and guarantee ourselves heavenly preservation.

BIOGRAPHY

Noah Manyika is the President of Salvation Now World Outreach and Senior Pastor of the Charlotte International Church .

He has been involved in several projects for community development in the Charlotte-Mecklenburg area of North Carolina, including the Brookstone Schools of Mecklenburg County, a network of private Christian schools for low-income children for which he was a founding board member.

He is a graduate of the Georgetown University School of Foreign Service in Washington D.C. where he was a Fulbright Scholar and student of former Secretary of State Madelaine Albright. He also holds a PhD in Christian Leadership.

Noah is married to Phillis, a partner with him in ministry, and they have been blessed with two daughters and a son.

QUICK ORDER FORM

Fax orders: 704-442-9236.

Telephone orders: Call 1-866-442-9236.

Email orders: orders@UplinkPublishing.com

Postal orders: Uplink Publishing, PO Box 32454,
Charlotte, NC 28232, USA.

Please send the following books, disks or reports.

_____

_____

_____

Please send more FREE information on:

❑ Other Books   ❑ Speaking/Seminars   ❑ Mailing Lists   ❑ Consulting

Name: _____

Address: _____

City: _____ State: _____ Zip: _____

Telephone: _____

Email address: _____

Sales tax: Please add 7% for products shipped to North Carolina addresses.

Shipping by air

U.S.: $4.00 for first book or disc and $2.00 for each additional product.
International: $9.00 for first book or disc: $5.00 for each additional product (estimate).

Payment: ❑ Check   ❑ Credit card:

❑ Visa ❑ MasterCard ❑ Discover ❑ Optima ❑ Amex

Card number: _____

Name on card: _____ Exp. Date: _____